In the Name of

IDENTITY

Violence and the Need to Belong

AMIN MAALOUF

Translated from the French by Barbara Bray

ARCADE PUBLISHING • NEW YORK

Arcade Publishing books may be purchased in bulk at special discounts for sales promotion, corporate gifts, fund-raising, or educational purposes. Special editions can also be created to specifications. For details, contact the Special Sales Department, Arcade Publishing, 307 West 36th Street, 11th Floor, New York, NY 10018 or arcade@skyhorsepublishing.com.

Arcade Publishing® is a registered trademark of Skyhorse Publishing, Inc.®, a Delaware corporation.

Visit our website at www.arcadepub.com.

10 9 8 7

Library of Congress Cataloging-in-Publication Data is available on file.

ISBN: 978-1-61145-324-9

Printed in the United States of America

for Andrée
for Ruchdi
for Tarek
for Ziad

Introduction

*H*OW MANY TIMES, since I left Lebanon in 1976 to live in France, have people asked me, with the best intentions in the world, whether I felt "more French" or "more Lebanese"? And I always give the same answer: "Both!" I say that not in the interests of fairness or balance, but because any other answer would be a lie. What makes me myself rather than anyone else is the very fact that I am poised between two countries, two or three languages and several cultural traditions. It is precisely this that defines my identity. Would I exist more authentically if I cut off a part of myself?

To those who ask the question, I patiently explain that I was born in Lebanon and lived there until I was 27; that Arabic is my mother tongue; that it was in Arabic translation that I first read Dumas and Dickens and *Gulliver's Travels;* and that it was in my native village, the village of my ancestors, that I experienced the pleasures of childhood and heard some of the stories that were later to inspire my novels. How could I forget all that? How could I cast it aside? On the other hand, I have lived for 22 years on the soil of France; I drink her water and wine; every day my hands touch her ancient stones; I write my books in her language; never again will she be a foreign country to me.

So am I half French and half Lebanese? Of course not. Identity can't be compartmentalised. You can't divide it up into halves or thirds or any other separate segments. I haven't got several identities: I've got just one, made up of many components in a mixture that is unique to me, just as other people's identity is unique to them as individuals.

Sometimes, after I've been giving a detailed account of exactly why I lay claim to all my affiliations, someone comes and pats me on the shoulder and says "Of course, of course — but what do you really feel, deep down inside?"

For a long time I found this oft-repeated question amusing, but it no longer makes me smile. It seems to reflect a view of humanity which, though it is widespread, is also in my opinion dangerous. It presupposes that "deep down inside" everyone there is just one affiliation that really matters, a kind of "fundamental truth" about each individual, an "essence" determined once and for all at birth, never to change thereafter. As if the rest, all the rest — a person's whole journey through time as a free agent; the beliefs he acquires in the course of that journey; his own individual tastes, sensibilities and affinities; in short his life itself — counted for nothing. And when, as happens so often nowadays, our contemporaries are exhorted to "assert their identity," they are meant to seek within themselves that same alleged fundamental allegiance, which is often religious,

national, racial or ethnic, and having located it they are supposed to flaunt it proudly in the face of others.

Anyone who claims a more complex identity is marginalised. But a young man born in France of Algerian parents
clearly carries within him two different allegiances or "belongings," and he ought to be allowed to use both. For the sake of
argument I refer to two "belongings," but in fact such a youth's
personality is made up of many more ingredients. Within him,
French, European and other western influences mingle with
Arab, Berber, African, Muslim and other sources, whether
with regard to language, beliefs, family relationships or to tastes
in cooking and the arts. This represents an enriching and fertile
experience if the young man in question feels free to live it
fully — if he is encouraged to accept it in all its diversity. But it
can be traumatic if whenever he claims to be French other
people look on him as a traitor or renegade, and if every time
he emphasises his ties with Algeria and its history, culture and
religion he meets with incomprehension, mistrust or even out-
right hostility.

The situation is even more difficult on the other side of the
Rhine. I'm thinking of the case of a Turk who might have
been born near Frankfurt 30 years ago and who has always
lived in Germany. He speaks and writes German better than
the language of his ancestors. Yet for the society of his
adopted country he isn't a German, while for that of his origins he is no longer completely a Turk. Common sense dic-
tates that he should be able to claim both allegiances. But at
present neither the law nor people's attitudes allows him to
accept his composite identity tranquilly.

I have quoted the first examples that came to mind, but I could have used many others. For instance, that of someone born in Belgrade of a Serbian mother and a Croatian father. That of a Hutu woman married to a Tutsi, or vice versa. Or that of an American with a black father and a Jewish mother.

It may be said that these are special cases. I don't agree. The handful of people I've cited are not the only ones with a complex identity. Every individual is a meeting ground for many different allegiances, and sometimes these loyalties conflict with one another and confront the person who harbours them with difficult choices. In some cases the situation is obvious at a glance; others need to be looked at more closely.

Is there any citizen of present-day Europe who doesn't sense a kind of tug-of-war, an inevitably ever-increasing conflict between on the one hand his affiliation to an ancient country like France, Spain, Denmark or England, and, on the other, his allegiance to the continental entity that is in the process of forming? And there are many dedicated "Europeans," from the Basque country to Scotland, who at the same time feel a strong and fundamental attachment to a particular region and its people, its history and its language. Can anyone in the United States even today assess his place in society without reference to his earlier connections, whether they be African, Hispanic, Irish, Jewish, Italian, Polish or other?

That said, I'm prepared to admit that the first examples I cited are to a certain extent special. All the people concerned in them are arenas for allegiances currently in violent conflict with one another: they live in a sort of frontier zone crisscrossed by ethnic, religious and other fault lines. But by virtue of this situation — peculiar rather than privileged — they have a special role to play in forging links, eliminating misunderstandings, making some parties more reasonable and others less belligerent, smoothing out difficulties, seeking compromise. Their role is to act as bridges, go-betweens, mediators between the various communities and cultures. And that is precisely why their dilemma is so significant: if they themselves cannot sustain their multiple allegiances, if they are continually being pressed to take sides or ordered to stay within their own tribe, then all of us have reason to be uneasy about the way the world is going.

I talk of their being "pressed" and "ordered" — but by whom? Not just by fanatics and xenophobes of all kinds, but also by you and me, by each and all of us. And we do so precisely because of habits of thought and expression deeply rooted in us all; because of a narrow, exclusive, bigoted, simplistic attitude that reduces identity in all its many aspects to one single affiliation, and one that is proclaimed in anger.

I feel like shouting aloud that this is how murderers are made — it's a recipe for massacres! That may sound somewhat extreme, but in the pages that follow I shall try to explain what I mean.

1

My Identity, My Allegiances

1

A LIFE SPENT WRITING has taught me to be wary of words. Those that seem clearest are often the most treacherous. "Identity" is one of those false friends. We all think we know what the word means and go on trusting it, even when it's slyly starting to say the opposite.

Far be it from me to want to keep on redefining the idea of identity. It has been the fundamental question of philosophy from Socrates's "Know thyself!" through countless other masters down to Freud. To approach it anew today would call for more qualifications than I possess and for very much greater temerity. The task I set myself is more modest. I want to try to understand why so many people commit crimes nowadays in the name of religious, ethnic, national or some other kind of identity. Has it always been like this since time immemorial, or is the present era influenced by hitherto unknown factors? Sometimes what I say may seem rather simplistic. If so it's because I want to set my argument out as calmly, patiently and fairly as possible, without resorting to jargon or unwarranted shortcuts.

What's known as an identity card carries the holder's family name, given name, date and place of birth, photograph, a list of certain physical features, the holder's signature and sometimes also his fingerprints — a whole array of details designed to prove without a shadow of doubt or confusion that the bearer of the document is so-and-so, and that amongst all the millions of other human beings there isn't one — not even his double or his twin brother — for whom he could be mistaken.

My identity is what prevents me from being identical to anybody else.

Defined in this way the word identity reflects a fairly precise idea — one which in theory should not give rise to confusion. Do we really need lengthy arguments to prove that there are not and cannot be two identical individuals? Even if in the near future someone manages, as we fear they may, to "clone" human beings, the clones would at best be identical only at the time of their "birth"; as soon as they started to live they would start being different.

Each individual's identity is made up of a number of elements, and these are clearly not restricted to the particulars set down in official records. Of course, for the great majority these factors include allegiance to a religious tradition; to a nationality — sometimes two; to a profession, an institution, or a particular social milieu. But the list is much longer than that; it is virtually unlimited. A person may feel a more or less strong attachment to a province, a village, a neighbourhood, a clan, a professional team or one connected with sport, a group of friends, a union, a company, a parish, a community of people with the same passions, the same sexual preferences, the same physical handicaps, or who have to deal with the same kind of pollution or other nuisance.

Of course, not all these allegiances are equally strong, at least at any given moment. But none is entirely insignificant, either. All are components of personality — we might almost call them "genes of the soul" so long as we remember that most of them are not innate.

While each of these elements may be found separately in many individuals, the same combination of them is never encountered in different people, and it's this that gives every individual richness and value and makes each human being unique and irreplaceable.

It can happen that some incident, a fortunate or unfortunate accident, even a chance encounter, influences our sense of identity more strongly than any ancient affiliation. Take the case of a Serbian man and a Muslim woman who met 20 years ago in a café in Sarajevo, fell in love and got married. They can never perceive their identity in the same way as does a couple that is entirely Serbian or entirely Muslim; their view of religion and mother country will never again be what it was before. Both partners will always carry within them the ties their parents handed down at birth, but these ties will henceforth be perceived differently and accorded a different importance.

Let us stay in Sarajevo and carry out an imaginary survey there. Let us observe a man of about 50 whom we see in the street.

In 1980 or thereabouts he might have said proudly and without hesitation, "I'm a Yugoslavian!" Questioned more closely, he could have said he was a citizen of the Federal Republic of Bosnia-Herzegovina, and, incidentally, that he came from a traditionally Muslim family.

If you had met the same man twelve years later, when the war was at its height, he might have answered automatically and emphatically, "I'm a Muslim!" He might even have grown the statutory beard. He would quickly have added that he was a Bosnian, and he would not have been pleased to be reminded of how proudly he once called himself a Yugoslavian.

If he was stopped and questioned now, he would say first of all that he was a Bosnian, then that he was a Muslim. He'd tell you he was just on his way to the mosque, but he'd also want you to know that his country is part of Europe and that he hopes it will one day be a member of the Union.

How will this same person want to define himself if we meet him in the same place 20 years hence? Which of his affiliations will he put first? The European? The Islamic? The Bosnian? Something else again? The Balkan connection, perhaps?

I shan't risk trying to predict. All these factors are part of his identity. He was born to a family that was traditionally Muslim; the language he speaks links him to the Southern Slavs, who were once joined together in a single state, but are so no longer; he lives on land which belonged sometimes to the Ottoman and sometimes to the Austrian Empire, and which played a part in the major dramas of European history. In every era one or other of his affiliations swelled up, so to speak, in such a way as to eclipse all the others and to appear to represent his whole identity. In the course of his life he'll have heard all kinds of fables. He'll have been told he was a proletarian pure and simple. Or a Yugoslavian through and through. Or, more recently, a Muslim. For a few difficult months he'll even have been made to think he had more in common with the inhabitants of Kabul than with those of Trieste!

In every age there have been people who considered that an individual had one overriding affiliation so much more important in every circumstance to all others that it might legitimately be called his "identity." For some it was the nation, for others religion or class. But one has only to look at the various conflicts being fought out all over the world today to realise that no one allegiance has absolute supremacy. Where people feel their faith is threatened, it is their religious affiliation that seems to reflect their whole identity. But if their mother tongue or their ethnic group is in danger, then they fight ferociously against their own co-religionists. Both the Turks and the Kurds are Muslims, though they speak different languages; but does that make the war between them any less bloody? Hutus and Tutsis alike are Catholics, and they speak the same language, but has that stopped them slaughtering one another? Czechs and Slovaks are all Catholics too, but does that help them live together?

I cite all these examples to underline the fact that while there is always a certain hierarchy among the elements that go to make up individual identities, that hierarchy is not immutable; it changes with time, and in so doing brings about fundamental changes in behaviour.

Moreover, the ties that count in people's lives are not always the allegedly major allegiances arising out of language, complexion, nationality, class or religion. Take the case of an Italian homosexual in the days of fascism. I imagine that for the man himself that particular aspect of his personality had up till then been important, but not more so than his professional activity, his political choices or his religious beliefs. But suddenly state repression swoops down on him and he feels threatened with humiliation, deportation or death. It's the recollection of certain books I've read and films I've seen that leads me to choose this example. This man, who a few years earlier was a patriot, perhaps even a nationalist, was no longer able to exult at the sight of the Italian army marching by; he may even have come to wish for its defeat. Because of the persecution to which he was subjected, his sexual preferences came to outweigh his other affiliations, among them even the nationalism which at that time was at its height. Only after the war, in a more tolerant Italy, would our man have felt entirely Italian once more.

The identity a person lays claim to is often based, in reverse, on that of his enemy. An Irish Catholic differentiates himself from Englishmen in the first place in terms of religion, but vis-à-vis the monarchy he will declare himself a republican; and while he may not know much Gaelic, at least he will speak his own form of English. A Catholic leader who spoke with an Oxford accent might seem almost a traitor.

One could find dozens of other examples to show how complex is the mechanism of identity: a complexity sometimes benign, but sometimes tragic. I shall quote various instances in the pages that follow, some briefly and others in more detail. Most of them relate to the region I myself come from — the Middle East, the Mediterranean, the Arab world, and first and foremost Lebanon. For that is a country where you are constantly having to question yourself about your affiliations, your origins, your relationships with others, and your possible place in the sun or in the shade.

2

I SOMETIMES FIND MYSELF "examining my identity" as other people examine their conscience. As you may imagine, my object is not to discover within myself some "essential" allegiance in which I may recognise myself. Rather the opposite: I scour my memory to find as many ingredients of my identity as I can. I then assemble and arrange them. I don't deny any of them.

I come from a family which originated in the southern part of the Arab world and which for centuries lived in the mountains of Lebanon. More recently, by a series of migrations, it has spread out to various other parts of the world, from Egypt to Brazil and from Cuba to Australia. It takes pride in having always been at once Arab and Christian, and this probably since the second or third century AD — that is, long before the rise of Islam and even before the West was converted to Christianity.

The fact of simultaneously being Christian and having as my mother tongue Arabic, the holy language of Islam, is one of the basic paradoxes that have shaped my own identity. Speaking Arabic creates bonds between me and all those who use it every day in their prayers, though most of them by far don't know it as well as I do. If you are in central Asia and meet an elderly scholar outside a Timuride *medersa,* you need only address him in Arabic for him to feel at ease. Then he will speak to you from the heart, as he'd never risk doing in Russian or English.

This language is common to us all — to him, to me and to more than a billion others. On the other hand, my being a Christian — regardless of whether I am so out of deep religious conviction or merely for sociological reasons — also creates a significant link between me and the two billion or so other Christians in the world. There are many things in which I differ from every Christian, every Arab and every Muslim, but between me and each of them there is also an undeniable kinship, in one case religious and intellectual and in the other linguistic and cultural.

That said, the fact of being at once an Arab and a Christian puts one in a very special situation: it makes you a member of a minority — a situation not always easy to accept. It marks a person deeply and permanently. I cannot deny that it has played a decisive part in most of the decisions I have had to make in the course of my own life, including my decision to write this book.

Thus, when I think about either of these two components of my identity separately, I feel close either through language or through religion to a good half of the human race. But when I take the same two elements together, I find myself face to face with my own specificity.

I could say the same thing about other ties. I share the fact that I'm French with 60 million or so others; the fact that I'm Lebanese with between eight and ten million, if you include the diaspora; but with how many do I share the fact that I'm both French and Lebanese? With a few thousand, at most.

Every one of my allegiances links me to a large number of people. But the more ties I have the rarer and more particular my own identity becomes.

If I went into my origins in more detail I'd have to say I was born into what is known as the Melchite or Greek Catholic community, which recognises the authority of the Pope while retaining some Byzantine rites. Seen from a distance, this affiliation is no more than a detail, a curiosity; but seen from close to, it is a defining aspect of my identity. In a country like Lebanon, where the more powerful communities have fought for a long time for their territory and their share of power, members of very small minorities like mine have seldom taken up arms, and have been the first to go into exile. Personally, I always declined to get involved in a war that struck me as absurd and suicidal; but this judgemental attitude, this distant way of looking at things, this refusal to fight, are not unconnected with the fact that I belong to a marginalised community.

So I am a Melchite. But if anyone ever bothered to look my name up in the administrative records — which in Lebanon, as you may imagine, classify people in terms of their religious persuasion — they would find me mentioned not among the Melchites, but in the register of Protestants. Why? It would take too long to explain. All I need say here is that in our family there were two rival family traditions, and that throughout my childhood I was a witness to this tug-of-war. A witness, and sometimes even the bone of contention too. If I was sent to the French school run by the Jesuit fathers it was because my mother, a determined Catholic, wanted to remove me from the Protestant influence prevailing at that time in my father's family, where the children were traditionally sent to British or American schools. It was because of this conflict that I came to speak French, and it was because I spoke French that during the war in Lebanon I went to live in Paris rather than in New York, Vancouver or London. It was for this reason, too, that when I started to write I wrote in French.

Shall I set out even more details about my identity? Shall I mention my Turkish grandmother, or her husband, who was a Maronite Christian from Egypt? Or my other grandfather, who died long before I was born and who I am told was a poet, a freethinker, perhaps a freemason, and in any case violently anti-clerical? Shall I go back as far as the great-great-great-uncle who was the first person to translate Molière into Arabic and to have his translation staged in 1848 in an Ottoman theatre?

No, there's no need to go on. I'll merely ask: how many of my fellow men share with me all the different elements that have shaped my identity and determined the main outlines of my life? Very few. Perhaps none at all. And that is what I want to emphasise: through each one of my affiliations, taken separately, I possess a certain kinship with a large number of my fellow human beings; but because of all these allegiances, taken together, I possess my own identity, completely different from any other.

I scarcely need exaggerate at all to say that I have some affiliations in common with every other human being. Yet no one else in the world has all or even most of the same allegiances as I do. Out of all the dozens of elements I can put forward, a mere handful would be enough to demonstrate my own particular identity, different from that of anybody else, even my own father or son.

I hesitated a long time before writing the pages that lead up to this one. Should I really start the book by describing my own situation at such length?

On the one hand, I wanted to use the example with which I was most familiar to show how, by adducing a few affiliations, one could simultaneously declare one's ties with one's fellow human beings and assert one's own uniqueness. On the other hand, I was well aware that the more one analyses a special case the more one risks being told that it *is* only a special case.

But in the end I took the plunge, in the belief that any person of goodwill trying to carry out his or her own "examination of identity" would soon, like me, discover that that identity is a special case. Mankind itself is made up of special cases. Life is a creator of differences. No "reproduction" is ever identical. Every individual without exception possesses a composite identity. He need only ask himself a few questions to uncover forgotten divergences and unsuspected ramifications, and to see that he is complex, unique and irreplaceable.

That is precisely what characterises each individual identity: it is complex, unique and irreplaceable, not to be confused with any other. If I emphasise this point it's because of the attitude, still widespread but in my view highly pernicious, which maintains that all anyone need do to proclaim his identity is simply say he's an Arab, or French, or black, or a Serb, or a Muslim, or a Jew. Anyone who sets out, as I have done, a number of affiliations, is immediately accused of wanting to "dissolve" his identity in a kind of undifferentiated and colourless soup. And yet what I'm trying to say is exactly the opposite: not that all human beings are the same, but that each one is different. No doubt a Serb is different from a Croat, but every Serb is also different from every other Serb, and every Croat is different from every other Croat. And if a Lebanese Christian is different from a Lebanese Muslim, I don't know any two Lebanese Christians who are identical, nor any two Muslims, any more than there are anywhere in the world two Frenchmen, two Africans, two Arabs or two Jews who are identical. People are not interchangeable, and often in the same family, whether it be Rwandan, Irish, Lebanese, Algerian or Bosnian, we find, between two brothers who have lived in the same environment, apparently small differences which make them act in diametrically opposite ways in matters relating to politics, religion and everyday life. These differences may even turn one of the brothers into a killer, and the other into a man of dialogue and conciliation.

Few would object explicitly to what I've been saying. Yet we all behave as if it were not true. Taking the line of least resistance, we lump the most different people together under the same heading. Taking the line of least resistance, we ascribe to them collective crimes, collective acts and opinions. "The Serbs have massacred . . . ," "The English have devastated . . . ," "The Jews have confiscated . . . ," "The Blacks have torched . . . ," "The Arabs refuse . . . ." We blithely express sweeping judgements on whole peoples, calling them "hardworking" and "ingenious," or "lazy," "touchy," "sly," "proud," or "obstinate." And sometimes this ends in bloodshed.

I know it is not realistic to expect all our contemporaries to change overnight the way they express themselves. But I think it is important for each of us to become aware that our words are not innocent and without consequence: they may help to perpetuate prejudices which history has shown to be perverse and deadly.

For it is often the way we look at other people that imprisons them within their own narrowest allegiances. And it is also the way we look at them that may set them free.

3

*I*DENTITY ISN'T GIVEN ONCE AND FOR ALL: it is built up and changes throughout a person's lifetime. This has been pointed out in numerous books and amply explained, but it is still worth emphasising again: not many of the elements that go to make up our identity are already in us at birth. A few physical characteristics of course — sex, colour and so on. And even at this point not everything is innate. Although, obviously, social environment doesn't determine sex, it does determine its significance. To be born a girl is not the same in Kabul as it is in Oslo: the condition of being a woman, like every other factor in a person's identity, is experienced differently in the two places.

The same could be said of colour. To be born black is a different matter according to whether you come into the world in New York, Lagos, Pretoria or Luanda. One might almost say that, from the point of view of identity, we're not even talking about the same colour in the different places. For an infant who first sees the light of day in Nigeria, the operative factor as regards his identity is not whether he is black rather than white, but whether he is Yoruba, say, rather than Hausa. In South Africa, whether a person is black or white is still a significant element in his identity, but at least equally meaningful is his ethnic affiliation, whether Zulu, Xhosa or something else. In the United States it's of no consequence whether you have a Yoruba rather than a Hausa ancestor: it's chiefly among the whites — the Italians, the English, the Irish and the rest — that ethnic origin has a determining effect on identity. Moreover, someone with both whites and blacks among his ancestors would be regarded as "black" in the United States, whereas in South Africa or Angola he would be considered as "of mixed race."

Why is the idea of mixed race taken into account in some countries and not in others? Why is ethnic affiliation a determining factor in some societies but not in the rest? One could put forward various more or less convincing answers to both questions. But that is not what concerns me at this stage. I mention these examples only to underline the fact that even colour and sex are not "absolute" ingredients of identity. That being so, all the other ingredients are even more relative.

To gauge what is really innate among the ingredients that go to make up identity, we may make use of a mental exercise which is extremely revealing. Imagine an infant removed immediately from its place of birth and set down in a different environment. Then compare the various "identities" the child might acquire in its new context, the battles it would now have to fight and those it would be spared. Needless to say, the child would have no recollection of his original religion, or of his country or language. And might he not one day find himself fighting to the death against those who ought to have been his nearest and dearest?

What determines a person's affiliation to a given group is essentially the influence of others: the influence of those about him — relatives, fellow-countrymen, co-religionists — who try to make him one of them; together with the influence of those on the other side, who do their best to exclude him. Each one of us has to make his way while choosing between the paths that are urged upon him and those that are forbidden or strewn with obstacles. He is not himself from the outset; nor does he just "grow aware" of what he is; he *becomes* what he is. He doesn't merely grow aware of his identity; he acquires it step by step.

The apprenticeship starts very soon, in early childhood. Deliberately or otherwise, those around him mould him, shape him, instil into him family beliefs, rituals, attitudes and conventions, together of course with his native language and also certain fears, aspirations, prejudices and grudges, not forgetting various feelings of affiliation and non-affiliation, belonging and not belonging.

And soon, at home, at school and in the next street, he will suffer his first knocks. By their words and by their looks, other people will make him feel he is poor, or lame, short or lanky, swarthy or too fair, circumcised or uncircumcised, or an orphan; those innumerable differences, major and minor, that define every personality and shape each individual's behaviour, opinions, fears and ambitions. Such factors may act as formative influences, but they can also cause permanent injuries.

———

It is these wounds that at every stage in life determine not only men's attitudes towards their affiliations but also the hierarchy that decides the relative importance of these ties. When someone has been bullied because of his religion, humiliated or mocked because of the colour of his skin, his accent or his shabby clothes, he will never forget it. Up till now I have stressed the fact that identity is made up of a number of allegiances. But it is just as necessary to emphasise that identity is also singular, something that we experience as a complete whole. A person's identity is not an assemblage of separate affiliations, nor a kind of loose patchwork; it is like a pattern drawn on a tightly stretched parchment. Touch just one part of it, just one allegiance, and the whole person will react, the whole drum will sound.

People often see themselves in terms of whichever one of their allegiances is most under attack. And sometimes, when a person doesn't have the strength to defend that allegiance, he hides it. Then it remains buried deep down in the dark, awaiting its revenge. But whether he accepts or conceals it, proclaims it discreetly or flaunts it, it is with that allegiance that the person concerned identifies. And then, whether it relates to colour, religion, language or class, it invades the person's whole identity. Other people who share the same allegiance sympathise; they all gather together, join forces, encourage one another, challenge "the other side." For them, "asserting their identity" inevitably becomes an act of courage, of liberation.

In the midst of any community that has been wounded, agitators naturally arise. Whether they are hot-heads or cool schemers, their intransigent speeches act as balm to their audience's wounds. They say one shouldn't beg others for respect: respect is a due and must be forced from those who would withhold it. They promise victory or vengeance, they inflame men's minds, sometimes they use extreme methods that some of their brothers may merely have dreamed of in secret. The scene is now set and the war can begin. Whatever happens "the others" will have deserved it. "We" can remember quite clearly "all they have made us suffer" since time immemorial: all the crimes, all the extortion, all the humiliations and fears, complete with names and dates and statistics.

I have lived in a country at war, in a neighbourhood being shelled from a nearby part of the same city. I have spent a night or two in a basement being used as an air-raid shelter, together with my young wife, who was pregnant, and my little son. From outside came the noise of explosions; inside, people exchanged rumours of imminent attack and stories about whole families being put to the sword. So I know very well that fear might make anyone take to crime. If, instead of mere rumours, there had been a real massacre in the neighbourhood where I lived, would I have remained calm and collected? If, instead of spending just a couple of days in that shelter, I had had to stay there for a month, would I have refused to take a gun if it had been put in my hand?

I prefer not to ask myself such questions too often. I had the good luck not to be put to the test; to emerge from the ordeal with my family unharmed, with my hands clean and with a clear conscience. But I speak of "good luck" because things could have turned out very differently if I'd been 16 instead of 26 when the war began in Lebanon. Or if I'd lost someone I loved. Or if I'd belonged to a different social class, or a different community.

After each new ethnic massacre we ask ourselves, quite rightly, how human beings can perpetrate such atrocities. Certain excesses seem incomprehensible; the logic behind them indecipherable. So we talk of murderous folly, of blood-thirsty ancestral or hereditary madness. In a way, we are right to talk of madness. When an otherwise normal man is transformed overnight into a killer, that is indeed insanity. But when there are thousands, millions of killers; when this phenomenon occurs in one country after another, in different cultures, among the faithful of all religions and among unbelievers alike, it's no longer enough to talk of madness. What we conveniently call "murderous folly" is the propensity of our fellow-creatures to turn into butchers when they suspect that their "tribe" is being threatened. The emotions of fear or insecurity don't always obey rational considerations. They may be exaggerated or even paranoid; but once a whole population is afraid, we are dealing with the reality of the fear rather than the reality of the threat.

I don't think any particular affiliation, be it ethnic, religious, national or anything else, predisposes anyone to murder. We have only to review the events of the last few years to see that any human community that feels humiliated or fears for its existence will tend to produce killers. And these killers will commit the most dreadful atrocities in the belief that they are right to do so and deserve the admiration of their fellows in this world and bliss in the next. There is a Mr. Hyde inside each one of us. What we have to do is prevent the conditions occurring that will bring the monster forth.

28

I shall not venture to propose a universal explanation of all the massacres, still less to suggest a miracle cure. I no more believe in simplistic solutions than I do in simplistic identities. The world is a complex machine that can't be dismantled with a screwdriver. But that shouldn't prevent us from observing, from trying to understand, from discussing, and sometimes suggesting a subject for reflection.

The theme that runs like a thread through the tapestry of this book might be formulated as follows: if the men of all countries, of all conditions and faiths can so easily be transformed into butchers, if fanatics of all kinds manage so easily to pass themselves off as defenders of identity, it's because the "tribal" concept of identity still prevalent all over the world facilitates such a distortion. It's a concept inherited from the conflicts of the past, and many of us would reject it if we examined it more closely. But we cling to it through habit, from lack of imagination or resignation, thus inadvertently contributing to the tragedies by which, tomorrow, we shall be genuinely shocked.

4

FROM THE VERY BEGINNING of this book I have been speaking of murderous or mortal identities. Identities that kill. The expression doesn't strike me as inappropriate insofar as the idea I'm challenging — the notion that reduces identity to one single affiliation — encourages people to adopt an attitude that is partial, sectarian, intolerant, domineering, sometimes suicidal, and frequently even changes them into killers or supporters of killers. Their view of the world is biased and distorted. Those who belong to the same community as we do are "ours," we like to think ourselves concerned about what happens to them, but we also allow ourselves to tyrannise over them: if they are thought to be "lukewarm" we denounce them, intimidate them, punish them as "traitors" and "renegades." As for the others, those on the opposite side, we never try to put ourselves in their place, we take good care not to ask ourselves whether on some point or other they might not be entirely in the wrong, and we won't let our hearts be softened by their complaints, their sufferings or the injustices that have been inflicted on them. The only thing that counts is the point of view of "our" side; a point of view that is often that of the most militant, the most demagogic and the most fanatical members of the community.

On the other hand, when one sees one's own identity as made up of a number of allegiances, some linked to an ethnic past and others not, some linked to a religious tradition and others not; when one observes in oneself, in one's origins and in the course one's life has taken, a number of different confluences and contributions, of different mixtures and influences, some of them quite subtle or even incompatible with one another; then one enters into a different relationship both with other people and with one's own "tribe." It's no longer just a question of "them" and "us": two armies in battle order preparing for the next confrontation, the next revenge match. From then on there are people on "our" side with whom I ultimately have little in common, while on "their" side there are some to whom I might feel very close.

But to return to the earlier state of mind, it's easy to imagine how it can drive people to the worst kind of extremities: if they feel that "others" represent a threat to their own ethnic group or religion or nation, anything they might do to ward off that danger seems to them entirely legitimate. Even when they commit massacres they are convinced they are merely doing what is necessary to save the lives of their nearest and dearest. And as this attitude is shared by those around them, the butchers often have a clear conscience and are amazed to hear themselves described as criminals. How can they be criminals when all they are doing is protecting their aged mothers, their brothers and sisters and children?

IN THE NAME OF IDENTITY

The feeling that they are fighting for the survival of their own loved ones and are supported by their prayers; the belief that if not in the present instance at least over the long term they can claim to be acting in legitimate self-defence: these characteristics are common to all those who in recent years, throughout the world, from Rwanda to former Yugoslavia, have committed the most abominable crimes.

We are not talking about isolated examples. The world is full of whole communities that are wounded — either enduring present persecution or still overshadowed by the memory of former sufferings — and who dream of exacting revenge. We cannot remain unmoved by their martyrdom; we can only sympathise with their desire to speak their own language freely, to practise their own religion without fear, and to preserve their own traditions. But compassion sometimes tends towards complaisance: those who have suffered from colonialist arrogance, racism and xenophobia are forgiven for excesses they themselves have committed because of their own nationalistic arrogance, their own racism and xenophobia. This attitude means we turn a blind eye to the fate of their victims, at least until rivers of blood have been shed.

The fact is, it's difficult to say where legitimate affirmation of identity ends and encroachment on the rights of others begins. Did I not say that the word identity was a "false friend"? It starts by reflecting a perfectly permissible aspiration, then before we know where we are it has become an instrument of war. The transition from one meaning to the other is imperceptible, almost natural, and sometimes we all just go along with it. We are denouncing an injustice, we are defending the rights of a suffering people — then the next day we find ourselves accomplices in a massacre.

All the massacres that have taken place in recent years, like most of the bloody wars, have been linked to complex and long-standing "cases" of identity. Sometimes the victims are forever desperately the same; sometimes the situation is reversed and the victimisers of yesterday become victims of today; or vice versa. Such words themselves, it must be said, are meaningful only to outside observers; for people directly involved in conflicts arising out of identity, for those who have suffered and been afraid, nothing else exists except "them" and "us," the insult and the atonement. "We" are necessarily and by definition innocent victims; "they" are necessarily guilty and have long been so, regardless of what they may be enduring at present.

And when we, the outside observers, go in for this game and cast one community in the role of the sheep and another in that of the wolf, what we are unwittingly doing is granting the former community impunity in advance for its crimes. In recent conflicts some factions have even committed atrocities against their own people, knowing that international opinion would automatically lay the blame on their opponents.

This first type of complacency carries with it another, equally unfortunate form, whereby, at each new massacre arising out of identity, the eternal sceptics immediately declare that things have been the same since the dawn of history, and that it would be naive and self-deluding to hope they might change. Ethnic massacres are sometimes treated, consciously or otherwise, like collective crimes of passion, regrettable but comprehensible, and anyway inevitable because they are "inherent in human nature."

The *laisser-tuer* attitude has already done great harm, and the realism invoked to justify it is in my opinion a misnomer. Unfortunately the "tribal" notion of identity is still the one most commonly accepted everywhere, not only amongst fanatics. But many ideas that have been commonly accepted for centuries are no longer admissible today, among them the "natural" ascendancy of men over women, the hierarchy between races, and even, closer to home, apartheid and the various other kinds of segregation. Torture, too, was for a long time regarded as a "normal" element in the execution of justice. For centuries, slavery seemed like a fact of life, and great minds of the past took care not to call it into question.

Then new ideas gradually managed to establish themselves: that every man had rights that must be defined and respected; that women should have the same rights as men; that nature too deserved to be protected; that the whole human race has interests in common in more and more areas — the environment, peace, international exchanges, the battle against the great scourges of disease and natural disaster; that others might and even should interfere in the internal affairs of countries where fundamental human rights are abused. And so on.

In other words, ideas that have hitherto prevailed throughout history are not necessarily those that ought to prevail in times to come. When new facts emerge we need to reconsider our attitudes and habits. Sometimes, when such facts emerge too rapidly, our mental attitudes can't keep up with them and we find ourselves trying to fight fires by pouring oil on them.

But in the age of globalisation and of the ever-accelerating intermingling of elements in which we are all caught up, a new concept of identity is needed, and needed urgently. We cannot be satisfied with forcing billions of bewildered human beings to choose between excessive assertion of their identity and the loss of their identity altogether, between fundamentalism and disintegration. But that is the logical consequence of the prevailing attitude on the subject. If our contemporaries are not encouraged to accept their multiple affiliations and allegiances; if they cannot reconcile their need for identity with an open and unprejudiced tolerance of other cultures; if they feel they have to choose between denial of the self and denial of the other — then we shall be bringing into being legions of the lost and hordes of bloodthirsty madmen.

But let us return for a moment to some examples I quoted at the beginning of this book. A man with a Serbian mother and a Croatian father, and who manages to accept his dual affiliation, will never take part in any form of ethnic "cleansing." A man with a Hutu mother and a Tutsi father, if he can accept the two "tributaries" that brought him into the world, will never be a party to butchery or genocide. And neither the Franco-Algerian lad, nor the young man of mixed German and Turkish origin whom I mentioned earlier, will ever be on the side of the fanatics if they succeed in living peacefully in the context of their own complex identity.

Here again it would be a mistake to see such examples as extreme or unusual. Wherever there are groups of human beings living side by side who differ from one another in religion, colour, language, ethnic origin or nationality; wherever there are tensions, more or less longstanding, more or less violent, between immigrants and local populations, Blacks and Whites, Catholics and Protestants, Jews and Arabs, Hindus and Sikhs, Lithuanians and Russians, Serbs and Albanians, Greeks and Turks, English-speaking and French-speaking Canadians, Flemings and Walloons, Chinese and Malays — yes, wherever there is a divided society, there are men and women bearing within them contradictory allegiances, people who live on the frontier between opposed communities, and whose very being might be said to be traversed by ethnic or religious or other fault lines.

We are not dealing with a handful of marginal people. There are thousands, millions of such men and women, and there will be more and more of them. They are frontier-dwellers by birth, or through the changes and chances of life, or by deliberate choice, and they can influence events and affect their course one way or the other. Those who can accept their diversity fully will hand on the torch between communities and cultures, will be a kind of mortar joining together and strengthening the societies in which they live. On the other hand, those who cannot accept their own diversity may be among the most virulent of those prepared to kill for the sake of identity, attacking those who embody that part of themselves which they would like to see forgotten. History contains many examples of such self-hatred.

5

NO DOUBT I SPEAK like a migrant and a member of a minority. But I think what I say reflects a sensibility that is more and more widely shared by our contemporaries. Isn't it a characteristic of the age we live in that it has made everyone in a way a migrant and a member of a minority? We all have to live in a universe bearing little resemblance to the place where we were born: we must all learn other languages, other modes of speech, other codes; and we all have the feeling that our own identity, as we have conceived of it since we were children, is threatened.

Many have left their native land, and many, though they haven't left it, can no longer recognise it. This may be partly due to the natural homesickness that is a permanent feature of the human soul; but it is also caused by an accelerated process of evolution which has made us travel further in 30 years than people used to go in many generations.

So to be a migrant no longer means merely belonging to a category of people who have been forced out of their native habitat; it has acquired a more general significance. The status of migrant itself is the first victim of a "tribal" notion of identity. If only one affiliation matters, if a choice absolutely has to be made, a migrant finds himself split and torn, condemned to betray either his country of origin or his country of adoption, and whichever course he follows the consequent betrayal is bound to cause him lasting bitterness and anger.

Before becoming an immigrant one is a migrant, an émigré. Before coming to one country one has had to leave another. And a person's feelings about the country he has left are never simple. If you have gone away, it is because there are things you have rejected — repression, insecurity, poverty, lack of opportunity. But this rejection is often accompanied by a sense of guilt. You are angry with yourself for abandoning loved ones, or the house you grew up in, or countless pleasant memories. And some ties linger on: those of language, religion, music; those with your companions in exile; those celebrated special holidays; those connected with cooking and food.

Similarly, one's feelings towards one's country of adoption are also ambiguous. If you have come here it's because you hope for a better life for yourself and your family. But this expectation is tinged with apprehension about the unknown — the more so because you are at a disadvantage in various ways, afraid of being rejected or humiliated, and on the look-out for signs of contempt, sarcasm or pity.

One's first reflex is not to flaunt one's difference but to try to pass unnoticed. The secret dream of most migrants is to be taken for "natives." Their first temptation is to imitate their hosts, and sometimes they succeed in doing so. But more often they fail. They haven't got the right accent, the right shade of skin, the right first name, the right family name or the proper papers, so they are soon found out. A lot of them know it's no use even trying, and out of pride or bravado make themselves out to be more different than they really are. And needless to say some go even further, and their frustration turns into violent contestation.

If I dwell on the migrant's state of mind it is not only because his dilemma is familiar to me personally. It is also because in this connection, more than in others, tensions arising out of identity can lead to the most lethal aberrations.

In the many countries where a native population with its own local culture lives side by side with another, more recently arrived population with different traditions, tensions arise that not only influence the behaviour of individuals but also affect the atmosphere prevailing in society as a whole and have an impact on political debate. This makes it all the more necessary to take a calm and judicious view of these highly emotional questions.

Wisdom is a view from on high, from the narrow path between two precipices, two extreme ideas. In the matter of immigration, the first of these extreme ideas is that which regards the host country as a blank sheet of paper on which everyone can write whatever he pleases, or, worse, as a waste-land where everyone can set up house with all his own impedimenta without making any changes in his habits or behaviour. The other extreme idea sees the host country as a page already written and printed, a land where the laws, values, beliefs and other human and cultural characteristics have been fixed once and for all, and where all that immigrants can do is conform to them.

Both notions strike me as equally unrealistic, sterile and harmful. Have I caricatured them? Unfortunately, I think not. Even if I had, caricature can serve a useful purpose if it helps people see how absurd an attitude can be if pushed to merely logical conclusions. Some will go on clinging to their own notions, but men of good sense will take a step towards the self-evident common ground: the fact that a host country is neither a tabula rasa, nor a fait accompli, but a page in the process of being written.

Its history must be respected. And when I say history I speak as a lover of History with a capital H. For me, it is not synonymous with empty nostalgia or indiscriminate worship of the past. On the contrary, it stands for all that has been built up over the centuries: memory, symbols, institutions, language, works of art, and all the other things to which one may legitimately be attached. At the same time, everyone will admit that a country's future cannot be a mere continuation of its history. It would be terrible for any country to have more reverence for its past than for its future. While that future should be constructed in a certain spirit of continuity it should also incorporate profound changes, together with significant contributions from elsewhere, as was the case in all the great eras of the past.

Have I merely been listing self-evident truths with which everybody agrees? Perhaps. But if tensions still exist and are even getting worse, it must be because those truths are neither self-evident enough nor really generally accepted.

What I am trying to prise out of these often confused considerations is not an intellectual consensus but a code of conduct, or at least a kind of safety barrier for everyone to use.

I insist on the fact that it is for everyone. My approach constantly calls for reciprocity, and this out of a concern for both fairness and efficiency. It's in this spirit that I would first say to the one party: "The more you steep yourself in the culture of the host country the more you will be able to steep yourself in your own"; and then, to the other party: "The more an immigrant feels that his own culture is respected, the more open he will be to the culture of the host country."

I set out the two equations in the same breath because they support one another, inseparable as the two parts of a ladder. Or, more prosaically, like clauses in a contract. For that is what we are really talking about — a moral contract, the elements of which need to be defined in each case to which it is applied: what, in the culture of a host country, is the minimum equipment that everyone is supposed to possess, and what may legitimately be challenged or rejected? The same question may be asked about the immigrants' own original culture: which parts of it deserve to be transmitted like a valuable dowry to the country of adoption, and which — which habits? which practices? — ought to be left behind at the door?

Such questions need to be asked, and everyone should make an effort to consider each one separately, even if the answers arrived at will never be entirely satisfactory. I live in France, but I wouldn't venture to list those parts of her heritage that ought to be adopted by anyone who wanted to live there. Everything I might suggest, whether a republican principle, an aspect of the French way of life, an outstanding person or a significant place — yes, everything I proposed, without exception, could justifiably be challenged. But it would be wrong to conclude from this that everything may be rejected out of hand. A fact may be vague, elusive and variable, but that doesn't mean it doesn't exist.

Again, the key word is reciprocity. If I try to belong to my country of adoption, if I now regard it as my own country and consider it part of me and myself part of it, and if I act accordingly, then I have the right to criticise every aspect of it. Similarly, if it respects me, if it recognises what I bring to it and regards me and my characteristics as now being part of itself, then it has the right to reject aspects of my culture that might be incompatible with its own way of life or with the spirit of its own institutions.

But the right to criticise someone else has to be won, deserved. If, in general, you treat another with hostility or contempt, your slightest adverse remark, whether justified or not, will be seen as a sign of aggression, much more likely to make him obstinate and unapproachable than to persuade him to change for the better.

Conversely, if you show someone friendship, sympathy and consideration, not merely superficially but in a manner that is sincere and felt to be so, then you may allow yourself to criticise, with some hope of being heard, things about him that you regard as open to objection.

Am I thinking of controversies like that which has arisen in various countries over the "Islamic veil"? These are not my main concern. But I am sure problems of that kind would be resolved more easily if relations with immigrants were approached in a different spirit. When someone feels that his language is despised, his religion ridiculed and his culture disparaged, he is likely to react by flaunting the signs of his difference. When someone feels he has a place in the country where he has chosen to live, then he will behave in quite another manner.

To approach someone else convincingly you must do so with open arms and head held high, and your arms can't be open unless your head *is* held high. If, every time you do approach another you feel you are betraying both your own people and yourself, your advances are doomed to failure. If I study someone else's language but he doesn't respect mine, to go on speaking his tongue ceases to be a token of amity and becomes an act of servitude and submission.

But to go back for a moment to the wearing of the veil, I don't doubt that this is an example of reactionary, backward-looking behaviour. I could explain at length why I take this attitude — because of my own convictions, and in the light not only of certain episodes in the history of the Arab-Muslim world but also of the long battle for emancipation being fought by the women there. But lengthy explanations would be pointless. That is not the real question. The real question isn't whether we are dealing with a conflict between ancient and modern, but why, in the course of human history, modernity is sometimes rejected: why it isn't always seen as progress and as a welcome development.

In any consideration of identity that question is essential, nowadays more than ever. And in this respect the Arab world is a very instructive example.

2

Modernity and "the Other"

1

ANYONE WHO IS FASCINATED, attracted, disturbed, horrified or intrigued by the Arab world is bound from time to time to ask himself certain questions.

Why those veils, those chadors, those dreary beards, those calls for assassination? Why so many manifestations of conservatism and violence? Are all these things inherent in such societies, in their culture and religion? Is Islam incompatible with liberty, democracy, the rights of man and of woman, with modernity itself?

Such questions are quite natural, and deserve better answers than the over-simplifications they usually receive. And these they receive from both sides — a favourite expression of mine, as you will have noticed. I must emphasise that inadequate answers come from both sides. I can't go along with the people who keep repeating the same old prejudices against Islam, and who whenever something particularly revolting occurs feel entitled to draw dismissive conclusions about the nature of certain peoples and their religion. At the same time I don't feel at ease, either, with the laboured excuses of those who reiterate without batting an eyelid that everything that happens is the result of some unfortunate misunderstanding, and that religion is synonymous with tolerance. Their motives do them honour, but while I don't put them on the same plane as the people who generate hatred, I don't find their views any more satisfactory.

When something reprehensible is done in the name of a doctrine of whatever kind, that doesn't automatically make the doctrine itself guilty, even if it can't be regarded as entirely unconnected with the deed in question. For example, by what right could I claim that the Taliban in Afghanistan have nothing to do with Islam, nor Pol Pot with Marxism, nor Pinochet's regime with Christianity? As an observer I am forced to conclude that each of these cases exhibits one possible application of the doctrine in question — not the only nor even the most widespread one, but however vexatious the example, it can't just be set aside. It is too facile, when things go wrong, to say such an outcome was inevitable, just as it is absurd to try to show that it was purely an accident that ought never to have happened. If it did happen, that was because it was to some degree probable.

It is perfectly permissible for someone who adheres to a certain system of beliefs to say he is at home with one interpretation of its doctrine and not with another. A faithful Muslim may think the behaviour of the Taliban contradicts — or does not contradict — both the letter and the spirit of his religion. I, who am not a Muslim and who moreover stand deliberately outside any system of belief, do not feel entitled to say what is and what is not consonant with

Islam. Of course I have my own hopes and preferences and point of view. I am frequently even tempted to say that this or that kind of extreme behaviour — planting bombs, banning music, legalising female circumcision — is inconsistent with my interpretation of Islam. But my interpretation of Islam is of no importance. Even if I were a most pious and erudite doctor of the Law my opinion would not put a stop to any controversy.

There will always be different and even contradictory interpretations, however much people study the scriptures, consult the commentators or set out the various arguments. The same authorities may be cited to tolerate or to condemn slavery, to venerate icons or burn them, to ban wine or allow it, to advocate either democracy or theocracy. Over the centuries, all human societies have managed to find religious quotations that seem to justify their current practices. It took two or three thousand years for the Christian and Jewish societies, which both claim the authority of the Bible, to start seeing that the precept "Thou shalt not kill" might apply to capital punishment; but a hundred years hence we'll be told it was self-evident. The text doesn't change; what changes is the way we look at it. But the text affects reality only through the medium of our view of it, and in every era the eye dwells on certain phrases and skims over others without taking them in.

For this reason it seems to me there's no point in racking one's brains over "the real message" of Christianity, Islam or Marxism. If you are looking for answers and not just for confirmation of the prejudices, positive or negative, that you carry within you, instead of pondering the essence of a doctrine you need to look at the behaviour, through the course of history, of those who claim to believe in it.

Is Christianity essentially tolerant, respectful of liberties and inclined towards democracy? If you framed the question like that, the answer would have to be "no." One only has to look through a few history books to see that throughout the last 2000 years torture, persecution and murder have been carried out on a massive scale in the name of that religion, and that the highest ecclesiastical authorities, as well as the overwhelming majority of ordinary believers, accepted the slave trade, the subjection of women, the most heinous dictatorships and the Inquisition itself. Does that mean Christianity is essentially despotic, racist, reactionary and intolerant? Not at all. You have only to look around you to see that it now lives comfortably with free speech, human rights and democracy. So should we conclude that the essence of Christianity has changed? Or that the "democratic spirit" that inhabits it now remained hidden for 1900 years, only to burst forth in the middle of the twentieth century?

If you want to understand all this you obviously need to frame your questions differently. Has democracy been a permanent requirement of Christianity throughout its history? The answer is clearly "no." But has democracy managed nevertheless to establish itself in societies belonging to the Christian tradition? Here the answer is equally clearly "yes." So when and how did this come about? To this question — and a similar one could equally reasonably be asked of Islam — the answer cannot be as brief as the replies to our previous queries. But it is one of the questions that we may reasonably try to address. All I shall say here is that the introduction into the world of a society that respects liberty in its various forms has been gradual and incomplete, and, in the context of history as a whole, extremely tardy. And while the Churches have taken note of this evolution, they have usually gone along with it more or less reluctantly rather than encouraging it. The impetus toward liberty has often come from people who stood quite apart from religious thinking.

My last remarks may have pleased those who have no love for religion. But I must remind them that the worst calamities of the twentieth century as regards despotism, persecution and the annihilation of freedom and human dignity derived not from religious but from quite other kinds of fanaticism. Some, like Stalinism, posed as the destroyers of religion; others, like Nazism and some other nationalist doctrines, simply turned their backs on it. It is true that since the 1970s religious fanaticism seems to have done its best to make up for lost time in the matter of horrors; but it still has a long way to go.

The twentieth century will have taught us that no doctrine in itself is necessarily a liberating force: all of them may be perverted or take a wrong turning; all have blood on their hands — communism, liberalism, nationalism, each of the great religions, and even secularism. Nobody has a monopoly on fanaticism; nobody has a monopoly on humane values.

If we want to take a new and worthwhile look at these sensitive matters we need to be scrupulously fair at every stage of our investigation. We need to avoid both hostility and complaisance, and above all the insufferable condescension that seems to have become second nature to some in the West and elsewhere.

2

*F*OR CENTURIES TWO ZONES OF CIVILISATION have rubbed shoulders with and confronted each other, one to the north and the other to the south and the east of the Mediterranean. I don't intend to dwell on the genesis of this division, but whenever one is talking of history it is relevant to remember that everything has a beginning, a middle, and, eventually, an end. In the days of Rome's supremacy, all the countries that subsequently became Christian, Muslim or Jewish belonged to the same empire: Syria was no less Roman than Gaul, and North Africa was certainly, from the cultural point of view, more Greco-Roman than northern Europe.

Things changed radically with the emergence, one after the other, of two conquering monotheisms. In the fourth century AD, Christianity became the official religion of the Roman Empire. After having begun by propagating their new faith through preaching, prayer and the example of the holy martyrs, the Christians went on to make ample use of power to consolidate their authority and exercise total control: they outlawed the ancient Roman religion and hunted down its last followers. Before long the limits of the Christian world were almost conterminous with the frontiers of the Empire, but these borders had become more and more uncertain: Rome was fated to "fall to the barbarians," as the old books put it in the fifth century.

Byzantium, the eastern capital, survived for another thousand years or so, but its attempt to reconstruct the Empire failed. Justinian did manage for a while to retake a fair amount of the territory that had been abandoned in Italy, Spain and North Africa. But in vain. His ambition was doomed to failure. His generals were not up to the task of defending the recovered provinces, and his death in AD 565 marked the end of an era and the death of an illusion. The great Roman Empire would never rise from its ashes. The Mediterranean would never more be united under one authority. Never again would the inhabitants of Barcelona, Lyons, Rome, Tripoli, Alexandria, Jerusalem and Constantinople all address their requests to one ruler.

Five years later, in AD 570, Mohammed, Mahomet, the Prophet of Islam, was born — outside the Empire, but not all that far away. Caravans of camels continually came and went between Mecca, the town where he was born, and cities of the Roman world such as Damascus and Palmyra. They also went back and forth between Arabia and the Persian Empire of the Sassanids, a rival of Roman power that was itself being shaken by strange convulsions.

I won't attempt to explain the mystical and religious phenomenon that is the message of Islam, which emerged under circumstances both complex and elusive. But it may be said with certainty that from the political point of view there was at the time a vacuum that favoured the advent of a new reality. For the first time in more than six centuries — that is, on the scale of human memory, since time immemorial — the greatness that was Rome no longer cast a shadow. As a result, many peoples felt both free and orphaned.

The vacuum — or perhaps it should rather be called an indraught — that allowed the Germanic tribes to spread across Europe, carving out for themselves territories that would later be called Saxony or the kingdom of the Franks, also allowed the tribes of Arabia to make a notable "sortie" out of the desert of their origins. In a few decades the Bedouins, who had till then lived on the margins of history, managed to make themselves masters of a vast expanse of territory stretching from Spain to the East Indies. And they did so in an amazingly orderly manner, with a fair amount of respect for others and without too much gratuitous violence.

Far be it from me to present that conquest as a peaceful advance, or to depict the Muslim world as a paradise of tolerance. But behaviour must be judged in relation to its time, and there is no doubt that Islam has traditionally managed to come to terms with the presence, in the areas under its control, of believers in other monotheistic religions.

But what, my opponents will say, is the point of praising the past when the present is as it is? In a way I agree with them. It's a poor consolation to know Islam was tolerant in the eighth century if today priests have their throats cut, intellectuals are stabbed and tourists machine-gunned. When I refer to the past I am not trying in the least to gloss over the atrocities that are thrown in our face every day by the news, in the form of reports and pictures from Algiers, Kabul, Teheran, Upper Egypt or elsewhere. My aim is quite different, and I want to make it plain: what I am fighting against, and always will, is the idea that on the one hand there's a religion — Christianity — destined for ever to act as a vector for modernism, freedom, tolerance and democracy, and on the other hand another religion — Islam — doomed from the outset to despotism and obscurantism. Such a notion is both wrong and dangerous, and throws a cloud over the future of a large part of the human race.

I have never renounced the faith of my fathers. I lay claim to this affiliation as well, and have no hesitation about acknowledging the influence it has had on my life. I was born in 1949, and have known essentially only a Church that is relatively tolerant, open to dialogue and capable of calling itself into question. So while I am indifferent to dogma and sceptical about certain attitudes, I regard this inherited allegiance as an enrichment, a spur to open-mindedness, and in no sense a kind of castration. I don't even ask myself whether the Church itself sees me as a believer: for me, a believer is simply someone who has faith in certain values. And these I would reduce to a single one: human dignity. The rest is merely hope or myth.

To sum up, I regard the Church as *fréquentable* — an institution one can associate with. If I'd been born a hundred years earlier I would probably have turned my back on it, judging it to be irremediably hostile to ideas of progress and liberty, and committed once and for all to bigotry and the status quo. That's why it is so important to evaluate the behaviour of men and institutions in relation to the context of history. Like many another I am appalled by what I see and hear in the Muslim world nowadays. But I am saddened too by those who seem to take pleasure in declaring that such things are in the nature of Islam, and that this state of affairs will never change.

No religion is completely devoid of intolerance, but if we were to draw up a comparison between the two "rival" faiths we would see that Islam doesn't come out of it too badly. If my ancestors had been Muslims in a country conquered by Christian armies, instead of Christians in a country conquered by the forces of Islam, I don't think they would have been allowed to live in their towns and villages, retaining their own religion, for over a thousand years. What in fact happened to the Muslims in Spain? Or those in Sicily? They were all done away with, to the last man, either murdered, driven into exile or forcibly baptised.

From the outset, and ever since, the history of Islam has reflected a remarkable ability to coexist with others. At the end of the nineteenth century the population of Istanbul, capital of the chief Muslim state at the time, contained a majority of non-Muslims — mostly Greeks, Armenians and Jews. Could we imagine Paris, London, Vienna or Berlin, at the same period, with a good half of their population made up of non-Christians, whether Muslims or Jews? Even today many Europeans would be shocked to hear the muezzin's call to prayer floating out over their cities.

I refrain from passing judgement. I merely observe that the history of Islam exhibits a long tradition of tolerance and coexistence among its practitioners. I hasten to add that in my view tolerance alone is not enough. I don't want to be tolerated: I insist on being treated as a fully-fledged citizen whatever my beliefs, whether I'm a Christian or a Jew in a country where the majority is Muslim, or a Muslim in the midst of Christians and Jews. And also if I have no religion at all. The idea that all the "people of the Book," i.e., the communities whose traditional faith is based on the Bible, should receive protection from the Muslims is no longer acceptable nowadays. It involves a status of inferiority, and that has never been exempt from humiliation.

But we ought to compare like with like. Islam established a "protocol of tolerance" at a time when Christian societies tolerated nothing, and for centuries this protocol embodied the most advanced form of coexistence in the whole world. It was perhaps in Amsterdam, in the middle of the seventeenth century, or in England a little later, that a different attitude began to emerge that was closer to our own conception of liberty of conscience. It was at the end of the eighteenth century that Condorcet, in France, advocated the "emancipation" of the Jews. Not until the second half of the twentieth century, and after the horrors we know all too well, did the position of religious minorities in Christian Europe finally undergo significant, and it is to be hoped irreversible, improvement.

These developments set new standards to which the "protocol of tolerance" that had previously prevailed in the Muslim countries did not conform. So has it been updated, modernised, adapted? In the main, no. It might even be said that the principles of that tolerance, instead of being brought into closer conformity with the expectations of our contemporaries, have sometimes been revised downwards. So that the Muslim world, for centuries a leader in the matter of tolerance, now finds itself lagging behind. But this reversal of the "moral balance of power" as between the north and the south of the Mediterranean is recent, very recent, and not as complete as some seem to believe.

Here again there are two opinions that need to be refuted. The first maintains that because the historical balance sheet of the Muslim world shows, all in all, a positive result, its present-day excesses are no more than temporary episodes. The second, conversely, sees contemporary intolerance and remembers a more broadminded past, but draws no practical conclusions. Both attitudes strike me as absurd. For me, history as a whole demonstrates that Islam has immense potentialities for coexistence and fruitful interaction with other cultures. But recent history shows that regression is possible too, and that potentialities could remain no more than potentialities for a long while.

I could go even further without much risk of exaggeration. If we drew up a comparative history of the Christian and the Muslim worlds, we would discover on the one hand a religion which was for a long while intolerant, with a clear tendency towards totalitarianism, but which has gradually been transformed into a religion of openness; and on the other hand, we would find a religion with a vocation for openness which has gradually drifted towards practices that are intolerant and totalitarian.

I could quote many examples recalling the fate of the Cathars, the Huguenots and the Jews and showing how both monotheisms have treated those they regarded as heretics, schismatics or infidels. But this isn't a history book, still less a collection of paradoxes. One question bothers me, however, when I compare the two historical paths: why has development in this context been so positive in the West and so disappointing in the Muslim world? To press the question and put it more precisely, why has the Christian West, which has a long tradition of intolerance and has always found it difficult to coexist with "the Other," produced societies that respect freedom of expression, whereas the Muslim world, which has long practised coexistence, now looks like a stronghold of fanaticism?

3

I HAVE MADE IT CLEAR that I don't subscribe to the opinion, so widely held in the West, that conveniently sees the Muslim religion as the source of all the evils afflicting Muslim societies. Nor, as I have already had occasion to note, do I think a religion can be entirely dissociated from the fate of its followers. But it does seem to me that the influence of religion on people is often exaggerated, while the influence of people on religion is neglected.

This is true of all bodies of belief. If it is in order to examine what effect communism has had on Russia, it is equally instructive to ask what effect Russia has had on communism, and how different the evolution of that doctrine, its place in history and its impact on other parts of the world would have been if it had come to power in Germany, England or France instead of Russia and China. We can imagine that a Stalin might have been born in Heidelberg, Leeds or Bordeaux. But we can just as easily imagine that there might never have been a Stalin at all.

Similarly, we may wonder what would have happened to Christianity if it had not triumphed in Rome — if it had not been implanted in a region steeped in the Roman law and Greek philosophy that are now regarded as the pillars of Western Christian civilisation, though both had reached their peak long before the emergence of Christianity.

This is not to deny the merits of my Western co-religionists. I just want to point out that if Christianity shaped Europe, Europe also shaped Christianity. Christianity today is what European societies have made of it. These societies have been transformed physically and intellectually, and in the process they have transformed their Christianity. How many times has the Catholic Church felt harassed, betrayed, ill-used! How often has it dug in its heels, trying to put off changes it believed to be contrary to faith, morals and the will of God! It has often lost out; but, without knowing it, it was really winning. Constantly forced to call itself into question, confronted with a victorious science that seemed to be challenging the Scriptures, faced with secular and republican ideas, the emancipation of women, the growing acceptability of premarital sex, births out of wedlock, contraception and thousands of other "diabolical innovations," the Church has always begun by resisting, and then gone on to accommodate itself and adapt.

Has the Church betrayed itself? People have often thought as much, and the future will no doubt offer them other occasions to do so. But the truth is that in this way Western society has created, through countless little touches of the chisel, a Church and a religion that can support men and women on the unprecedented journey they are embarked upon today.

Western society has invented the Church and the religion it needed. I use the word "need" in the widest possible sense, which includes the thirst for spirituality. All society has taken part in the process — believers and unbelievers alike; anyone who has contributed to the evolution of mental attitudes has also contributed to the evolution of Christianity. And since history goes on going on, they will go on contributing.

In the Muslim world, too, society has always produced a religion in its own image. This image has never been the same, though, from one era to another, nor from one country to another. When the Arabs were triumphant and felt the world was theirs for the taking, they interpreted their faith in a spirit of tolerance and openness. For example, they undertook an extensive programme of translation from the Greek, Persian and Indian traditions which led to a great advance in science and philosophy. At first, imitation and copying were considered sufficient, but then people found the courage to try new departures in astronomy, agronomy, chemistry, medicine and mathematics. The same thing happened in daily life — in the arts of gastronomy, fashion, hairdressing and singing. There were even "gurus" of fashion, the most famous of whom is still Ziryab.

It was not just a brief parenthesis. From the seventh to the fifteenth century Baghdad, Damascus, Cairo, Cordoba and Tunis all produced great scholars and thinkers as well as talented artists. Isfahan, Samarkand and Istanbul still brought forth great and beautiful works right up to the seventeenth century and sometimes beyond. Arabs were not the only contributors to this movement. Islam, from its beginnings, opened itself freely to the Iranians, Turks, Indians and Berbers. This has sometimes been judged unwise, as the Arabs were submerged and soon lost power in the empire they themselves had conquered. But that was the price that had to be paid for the universality proclaimed by Islam. Sometimes a horde of Turkmenian warriors would charge in from the steppes of central Asia: when they reached the gates of Baghdad they had only to utter the phrase signifying conversion — "There is no God but Allah, and Mohammed is His Prophet" — and no one could challenge their claim to belong to Islam. Soon after, they would also claim their share of power, sometimes with the overzealousness characteristic of converts. From the point of view of political stability this state of affairs could be disastrous; but it was a marvellous source of cultural enrichment. From the banks of the Indus to the Atlantic, the best minds could blossom under the protection of Arab civilisation. And this didn't apply only to those who subscribed to the new religion. In the case of translations, Christians were often called upon because they were more expert in Greek. And it is significant that Maimonides chose Arabic as the language in which to write his *Guide for the Perplexed,* one of the monuments of Jewish thought.

I don't claim that the picture I've just sketched of Islam is the only true one. Nor that it is more representative of Muslim doctrine than that of the Taliban, for example. But nor is it just a personal interpretation. In a few lines I have surveyed whole centuries, entire countries, which produced thousands upon thousands of different images of Islam. Baghdad in the ninth century was still sparkling with life;

Baghdad in the tenth century had become surly, bigoted and dreary. Cordoba, on the other hand, was at its peak in the tenth century, but by the beginning of the thirteenth had become a bastion of fanaticism: the Catholics were about to take possession, and the last Muslim defenders of the city would no longer tolerate dissenting voices.

This is a phenomenon to be seen in other periods, including our own. Whenever Muslim society has felt safe it has felt able to be open, and the image Islam presents of itself at such times is nothing like the caricatures of today. I don't claim that the older image is a more accurate reflection of the original spirit of Islam; merely that Islam, like any other religion or doctrine, always bears the marks of time and place. Societies that are sure of themselves are mirrored by a religion that is confident, serene and open; uncertain societies are reflected in a religion that is hypersensitive, sanctimonious and aloof. Dynamic societies have a dynamic Islam, one that is innovative and creative; sluggish societies have a sluggish Islam, one that resists all change.

But let us leave for the moment such contrasts between "good" and "bad" religion — they are bound to be simplistic — and concentrate on something more precise. When I refer to the influences of societies on religions I am thinking for example of the fact that when Muslims in the Third World attack the West, it is not only because they are Muslims and the West is Christian, but also because they are poor, downtrodden and derided, while the West is rich and powerful. I say "also," but I think "above all." For when I look at the militant Islamic movements of today I can easily detect, both in their words and in their methods, the Third World theories that became popular the 1960s; I certainly haven't been able to find any obvious precedent in the history of Islam itself. Such movements are not a product of Muslim history; they are a product of our time, with all its tensions, distortions, stratagems and despairs.

I do not propose to discuss the doctrine behind these movements here, nor do I ask whether or not it is consistent with Islam; I have already said what I think about such questions. What I am saying now is that while I can see quite clearly how such movements are the product of our troubled times, I cannot see how they could be the product of Muslim history. Watching Ayatollah Khomeini, surrounded by his Revolutionary Guards, asking his people to rely on their own strength, denouncing the "Great Satan" and vowing to remove all traces of Western culture, I couldn't help thinking of the elderly Mao Tse-tung of the Cultural Revolution, surrounded by his Red Guards, denouncing the "great paper tiger" and vowing to remove all traces of capitalist culture. I wouldn't say the two cases were identical, but I do see many similarities between them, whereas I don't see anybody in the history of Islam who reminds me of Khomeini. Nor, however carefully I look into the history of the Muslim world, do I find any mention of the setting up of an "Islamic republic" or the coming of an "Islamic revolution."

What I am objecting to here is the habit that people have got into, both in the North and in the South, and whether they are distant observers or zealous partisans, of classifying everything that happens in a Muslim country as related to Islam, whereas there are many other factors that are much more relevant. You could read a dozen large tomes on the history of Islam from its very beginnings and you still wouldn't understand what is going on in Algeria. But read 30 pages on colonialism and decolonisation and then you'll understand quite a lot.

4

*B*UT I WILL CLOSE THIS SHORT PARENTHESIS and return to my original theme: that too much emphasis is often laid on the influence of religions on people, and not enough on the influence of peoples and their history on religions. The influence is reciprocal, I know. Society shapes religion, and religion in its turn shapes society. But I have observed that because of a certain mental habit that we have got into we tend to see only one side of this dialectic, and the omission greatly distorts our perception.

Some people are always ready to blame Islam for all the dramatic episodes, past or present, that have occurred in Muslim societies. Not only is this attitude unfair; it also makes world events completely unintelligible.

For centuries similar things were said about Christianity, before it became clear that in the end Christianity was capable of modernising itself. I am sure this is also true of Islam. However, I can understand people's doubts. And I think it will take time, a long time, several generations perhaps, before we have proof that what we see happening in Algeria and Afghanistan and a lot of other places — that mixture of violence, atavism, despotism and repression — is no more intrinsic to Islam than the Inquisitors' burnings at the stake or the theory of divine right of kings were inseparable from Christianity.

The notion that Islam has always been a force against change is so deep-rooted I hardly dare to attack it. But it has to be done. Otherwise we can't get anywhere. If we resign ourselves to the idea that Islam dooms its adherents irremediably to inaction, and if we accept that these adherents — almost a quarter of the world's population — will never renounce their religion, then the future of our planet looks very depressing indeed. But I accept neither the hypothesis behind this argument nor its conclusion.

Yes, of course, there has been inaction and stagnation. Between the fifteenth and nineteenth centuries, while the West was making rapid advances, the Arab world marked time. Religion probably had something to do with this phenomenon, but it seems to me that it was primarily its victim. In the West, society modernised its religion; in the Muslim world that didn't happen. Not because Islam was not capable of being modernised — which hasn't been proved — but because in that part of the world society didn't modernise itself. That was because of Islam, some people will say. It's easily said. But was it Christianity that modernised Europe? Without going so far as to say that modernisation happened in spite of and against religion, we may reasonably argue that religion did not act as a driving force in the matter: on the contrary, it tended throughout to put up an often fierce resistance to it. The impetus for change had to be strong, profound and lasting in order to weaken religion's resistance and force it to adjust.

Such a destabilising but salutary impulse never made itself felt in the Muslim world. That extraordinary springtime of creative humanity; that total revolution — scientific, technological, industrial, intellectual and moral; that long, patient, detailed toil on the part of evolving peoples who every day experimented and invented, ceaselessly challenging old certainties and shaking up outdated attitudes — all this was not just some other event. It was something unique in history, the event that laid the foundations of the world as we know it today. And it took place in the West — in the West and nowhere else.

Why in the West and not in China, Japan, Russia or the Arab world? Did the change come about because of, or in spite of Christianity? Historians will go on exchanging theories on the subject for a long while. But what can scarcely be disputed is the fact itself: the emergence in the West in the course of the last few centuries of a civilisation that was to set physical and intellectual standards for the whole world, marginalising all other civilisations and reducing their status to that of peripheral cultures threatened with extinction.

At what moment did the predominance of Western civilisation become virtually irreversible? In the fifteenth century? Not before the eighteenth? But from my present point of view that doesn't matter. What is both certain and crucial is that one day a certain civilisation seized the reins of the planet. Its science became Science, its medicine Medicine, its philosophy Philosophy, and from then on that trend towards concentration and standardisation has not stopped.

On the contrary, it has gone on accelerating, spreading simultaneously to all fields of activity and all continents.

I insist on the point that we are dealing here with an event unprecedented in history. True, there had been times in the past when one civilisation — Egyptian, Mesopotamian, Chinese, Greek, Roman, Arab or Byzantine — seemed to be in advance of all the others. But what has been set in motion in Europe during the last few centuries is a completely different phenomenon. I see it as a kind of fertilisation. That is the only comparison that comes to mind: a lot of spermatozoa make for the ovule and one of them succeeds in piercing the membrane. All the other "suitors" are then rejected; henceforth there is just one "father," and it is him that the child will resemble. Why him and not another? Was this particular "suitor" superior in some ways to his neighbours and rivals? Was he healthier or more promising than the rest? Not necessarily; not in any obvious way. All kinds of factors are involved, some of them linked to ability, others to circumstance or chance.

But this isn't the most significant part of the comparison. What matters most is what comes next. The question is not so much why Aztec or Islamic or Chinese civilisation did not manage to become the dominant one — each of them had its hang-ups, its weaknesses, its strokes of bad luck. What we need to know is why, when European civilisation took the lead, all the others began to decline, and why they all became marginalised in a way that now seems irreversible. Probably — though this only begins to provide an answer — it was because mankind as a whole now had at its disposal the technical means of worldwide dominance. But let us leave aside for the moment the word dominance and say instead that mankind was ripe for the emergence of a worldwide civilisation. The egg was ready to be fertilised, and western Europe performed the deed.

To such effect that we have only to look around us to see that the West is everywhere: in Vladivostok as in Singapore, Boston, Dakar, Tashkent, São Paolo, Noumea, Jerusalem and Algiers. For half a millennium everything with a lasting effect on the ideas of men, their health, the landscape that surrounds them and their daily lives has been the work of the West. Capitalism, communism, fascism, psychoanalysis, ecology, electricity, aviation, automobiles, the atomic bomb, the telephone, television, computers, penicillin, the pill, human rights — and gas chambers. Yes, all of it, the weal of the world and its woe — all of it has come from the West.

Wherever on the planet one happens to live, all modernisation is now westernisation. And this trend is merely accentuated and accelerated by technical progress. True, monuments and other great achievements bearing the imprint of other civilisations are to be seen everywhere. But everything that is newly created — buildings, institutions, aids to knowledge or improvements to life-styles — all is produced in the image of the West.

This reality is experienced differently by those born in the dominant civilisation and those born outside it. The former can change, advance in life, adapt without ceasing to be themselves. One might even say that the more Westerners modernise themselves the more completely in harmony they feel with their culture. Only those among them who reject modernity find themselves out of touch.

For the rest of the world's inhabitants, all those born in the failed cultures, openness to change and modernity presents itself differently. For the Chinese, Africans, Japanese, Indians and American Indians, as for Greeks, Russians, Iranians, Arabs, Jews and Turks, modernisation has constantly meant the abandoning of part of themselves. Even though it has sometimes been embraced with enthusiasm, it has never been adopted without a certain bitterness, without a feeling of humiliation and defection. Without a piercing doubt about the dangers of assimilation. Without a profound identity crisis.

5

*W*HEN MODERNITY BEARS THE MARK OF "THE OTHER" it is not surprising if some people confronting it brandish symbols of atavism to assert their difference. This reaction may be seen today among some Muslims, men and women, but the phenomenon is not peculiar to one culture or religion.

For example, it wasn't until the Bolshevik revolution that Russia managed at last to abandon the old Julian calendar. Changing to the Gregorian calendar made people feel they were accepting the fact that in the almost immemorial war between Orthodoxy and Catholicism, the latter had had the last word.

That was only a symbol, you say? Everything in history is expressed in symbols — greatness and degradation, victory and defeat, happiness, prosperity, want. And above all identity. For a change to be accepted it isn't enough that it accords with the spirit of the age. It must also pass muster on the symbolic plane, without making those who are being asked to change feel they are betraying themselves.

In recent years, in France, I've noticed some of my closest friends tending to speak of globalisation as if it were a catastrophe. They are not as thrilled as they used to be at the idea of the "global village"; they are cool about the Internet and the latest advances in communications. This is because they now see globalisation as synonymous with Americanisation, and they wonder what future there will be for France in an increasingly standardised world, and what will become of France's language, culture, prestige, influence and way of life. They are vexed when a fast food store opens in their neighbourhood, they inveigh against Hollywood, CNN, Disney and Microsoft, and comb the newspapers for anything resembling an Anglicism.

I use this example because I think it shows how even in the West, even in a developed country universally respected and with a flourishing culture, modernisation becomes suspect as soon as it is perceived as a Trojan horse introduced by another culture that is both alien and overbearing.

It is all the easier to imagine the reactions of the various non-Western peoples whose every step, for many generations, has already been accompanied by a sense of defeat and self-betrayal. They have had to admit that their ways were out of date, that everything they produced was worthless compared with what was produced by the West, that their attachment to traditional medicine was superstitious, their military glory just a memory, the great men they had been brought up to revere — the poets, scholars, soldiers, saints and travellers — disregarded by the rest of the world, their religion suspected of barbarism, their language now studied only by a handful of specialists, while they had to learn other people's languages if they wanted to survive and work and remain in contact with the rest of mankind. Whenever they speak with a Westerner it is always in his language, almost never in their own. There are millions of people south and east of the Mediterranean who can speak English, French, Spanish and Italian. How many Englishmen, Frenchmen, Spaniards or Italians have thought it worthwhile to study Arabic or Turkish?

Yes, at every turn they meet with disappointment, disillusion or humiliation. How can their personalities fail to be damaged? How can they not feel their identities are threatened? That they are living in a world which belongs to others and obeys rules made by others, a world where they are orphans, strangers, intruders or pariahs? What can be done to prevent some of them feeling they have been bereft of everything and have nothing more to lose, so that they come, like Samson, to pray to God for the temple to collapse on top of them and their enemies alike?

I don't know if many hard-liners argue like this consciously. But they don't really need to. A wound doesn't have to be described in order to be felt.

It was towards the end of the eighteenth century that the Muslims living around the Mediterranean began to realise they were being marginalised and that there was a growing gulf between them and the West. It's never easy to date something as vague as a realisation, but it is generally accepted that it was after Napoleon's Egyptian campaign in 1799 that a number of people, men of letters and politicians alike, began asking themselves questions such as: Why have we got so left behind? Why is the West so advanced? How did they do it? What must we do to catch up?

For Mohammed (or Mehemet) Ali, viceroy of Egypt, the only way to catch up with Europe was to imitate it. He went a long way along this path, calling on European doctors to create a faculty of medicine in Cairo, rapidly introducing new agricultural and industrial techniques, and going so far as to entrust the command of his army to one of Napoleon's ex-officers. He even allowed some French Utopians — the Saint-Simonians — to carry out in Egypt some bold experiments that Europe wanted nothing to do with. In the course of a few years he made his country a respected regional power. The voluntarist westernisation that he promoted undoubtedly began to bear fruit. As resolutely as Peter the Great, but slightly less brutally and in the face of much less resistance, the former Ottoman dignitary seemed to be building in the East a modern state capable of taking an accepted place among the nations of the world.

But the dream shattered, and all it would bequeath to the Arabs was a bitter memory. Even today, intellectuals and political leaders still speak sadly, but also angrily, of that missed opportuniy, and are ready to explain to anyone who will listen that the European powers, who believed that Mohammed Ali was growing too dangerous and independent, got together to thwart his ambitions, going as far as to set up a joint military expedition against him. He ended his life vanquished and humiliated.

To tell the truth, when you step back in time and take a historical look at all the military and diplomatic manoeuvring surrounding this manifestation of the Eastern Question, you might reasonably conclude that it was merely an ordinary episode in the story of the balance of power. Great Britain preferred to have an ailing and weakened Ottoman Empire on the route to India rather than a strong and modern Egypt. This attitude wasn't fundamentally different from that which had led Britain to oppose Napoleon a few years before and to create a coalition capable of dismantling the European empire he had recently brought into being. But nineteenth-century Egypt can't be compared to France. France was already a great power: she might be beaten and appear down and out, but she could rise again prosperous and victorious a generation later. In 1815 France was vanquished and occupied. By 1830, just 15 years later, she had recovered sufficiently to try to conquer the vast territory of Algeria. But Egypt could not call upon such reserves. She was beginning to emerge from a long, a very long period of somnolence. She had just embarked on modernisation; and the blow inflicted upon her under Mohammed Ali proved fatal. She would never have another such opportunity to take the lead.

From this episode the Arabs concluded then and still conclude now that the West doesn't want the rest of the world to be like it; it just wants them to obey it. The correspondence between the ruler of Egypt and the chancelleries of the West contains poignant passages in which he doesn't hesitate to point out the "civilising mission" he had undertaken. After declaring that he had always respected the interests of the Europeans, he wonders why they should be trying to sacrifice him. "I am not of their religion," he writes, "but I too am a man, and I ought to be treated humanely."

6

*W*HAT THE CASE OF MOHAMMED ALI SHOWS is that in the Arab world modernisation was soon regarded as necessary, perhaps even a matter of urgency. But it has never been seen as something to be embarked upon calmly and without undue haste. Not only had the process to be carried out at top speed, whereas Europe was able to take into account its own cultural, social and religious hang-ups, but it also had to be brought about in the face of an insatiable and often contemptuous West that was itself expanding rapidly.

I have referred to Egypt, but I might just as easily have cited China, which at the same period was suffering under the infamous "Opium Wars," fought in the name of free trade because China refused to open itself up to the lucrative traffic in drugs. The fact is that the rise of the West, which made an incomparable contribution to the good of all mankind, also had its more shady aspects. The event that created the modern world was also an agent of destruction. The West, brimming over with energy, conscious of its new strength, convinced of its own superiority, had set out to conquer the world in all directions and in every field at once, spreading the benefits of medicine and new techniques as well as ideals of liberty. But at the same time it looted, massacred and brought people into subjection, arousing as much resentment as fascination everywhere.

I have briefly recalled these truths in order to underline the fact that it has never been easy for an Arab — or an Indian, a Madagascan or an Indochinese — to subscribe fully, without reservations, anguish or regrets, to the culture of the West. Many apprehensions and grievances have had to be overcome; sometimes pride has had to be swallowed or subtle compromises invented. It soon became impossible to wonder merely, as in the days of Mohammed Ali, "How can we modernise ourselves?" More complicated questions inevitably arose: "How can we modernise ourselves without losing our identity?"; "How can we assimilate Western culture without denying our own?"; "How can we acquire the West's knowledge without leaving ourselves at its mercy?"

The time had passed for the systematic and relatively unself-conscious westernisation practised by the ruler of Egypt. He was a man of another age. As in seventeenth-century France, where they had no hesitation about entrusting the government to the Italian Giulio Mazarini, or in eighteenth-century Russia, where a German woman could mount the throne of the Tsars, the generation of Mohammed Ali had thought not in terms of nationality but in terms of dynasties and states. He was himself of Albanian origin and there was no more reason why he should entrust the command of the Egyptian army to an Arab than to a Bosnian or a

Frenchman. His story reminds one of the Roman generals who built themselves a power base in some province of the Empire, but dreamed only of marching on Rome to proclaim themselves *imperator* and therefore august. If Mohammed Ali had been able to make his dream come true, it is in Istanbul that he would have installed himself, to make it the capital of a Europeanised Muslim empire.

But things had already changed by the time he died in 1849. Europe was entering a period of nationalism, and empires made up of many different nationalities were on the decline. The Muslim world was soon to follow this trend. In the Balkans, the peoples ruled over by the Ottomans were beginning to stir in the same way as those in the Austro-Hungarian Empire. The inhabitants of the Middle East too were now pondering their "true" identity. Hitherto, everyone had his or her own linguistic, religious or regional affiliations, but the problem of allegiance to a state did not arise: all were the subjects of the sultan. But once the Ottoman Empire started to disintegrate, there arose the question of the division of the spoils, with all the insoluble problems that it entailed. Should each community have its own state? But what if several communities had lived together for centuries in the same country? Should the Empire be split up on lines of language or religion, or in accordance with the traditional frontiers of its provinces? Those who have witnessed the breaking up of Yugoslavia over recent years may have some idea, on a very small scale, of what the liquidation of the Ottoman Empire must have been like.

All the various peoples involved did their best to blame the others for the ills that afflicted them. If the Arabs failed to make progress it was because of the paralysing domination of the Turks. If the Turks were backward, it was because for centuries they had had the millstone of the Arabs around their neck. Is it not the first duty of nationalism to find for every problem a culprit rather than a solution? So the Arabs threw off the Turkish yoke believing this would at last usher in their own renaissance, while the Turks undertook the "de-arabisation" of their culture, language, alphabet and costume in order to facilitate their incorporation into Europe.

There may have been some truth in all their arguments. What happens to us is often to some extent the fault of others, and for what happens to others we are always to some extent to blame. But no matter. If I mention the arguments of the Arab or Turkish nationalists, it is not to debate them, but rather to draw attention to a truth too often forgotten. Which is that the Muslim world's immediate response to the dilemma posed by the need for modernisation has not always been religious radicalism. For a long, a very long time, this remained the attitude of an extremely small and marginal, not to say insignificant, minority. The Muslim world of the Mediterranean was ruled over in the name not of religion but of nation. It was the nationalists who led these lands to independence. They were the fathers of their countries; it was they who in the decades that followed held the reins of power; it was towards them that all eyes turned in expectation and hope. Not all of them were as openly secular and modernist as Ataturk, but they made little reference to religion, which they had put to one side, so to speak.

The most important of these leaders was Nasser. Did I say "the most important"? That's a feeble understatement. It is hard to imagine now the sort of prestige the Egyptian president enjoyed after 1956. His photographs were everywhere, from Aden to Casablanca; his name was on the lips of young and old alike; loudspeakers blared out songs in praise of him; and when he delivered one of his lengthy speeches people would gather patiently around transistor radios for two or three or four hours at a time. He was a popular idol, a god. I haven't been able to find a parallel in all recent history. There is no one whose influence extended over so many countries at once and with such intensity. As far as the Arab-Muslim world is concerned, at least, there has never been another phenomenon remotely like it.

But Nasser, who more than anyone else represented the aspirations of Arabs and of Muslims in general, was a fierce enemy of the Islamists. They tried to assassinate him and he had several of their leaders executed. I remember, moreover, that in those days the man in the street regarded activists belonging to Islamic militant groups as enemies of the Arab nation, and often as "henchmen" of the West as well.

All this goes to show that when anyone sees political, anti-modernist and anti-western Islamism as the spontaneous and natural expression of the Arab peoples he is jumping to conclusions. It wasn't until the nationalist leaders, and Nasser above all, reached an impasse, partly through a series of military setbacks and partly because they were unable to solve the problems of underdevelopment, that a significant section of the population began to lend an ear to the voices of religious radicalism, and that, in the 1970s, beards and veils started to burgeon as signs of protest.

I could go on at length about Egypt, Algeria and the rest, describing the illusions and disillusions, the false starts and disastrously wrong choices, and the discomfiture of nationalism, socialism and everything else that the youth of the region, like the youth in the rest of the world, from Indonesia to Peru, believed in and then stopped believing in. But all I wanted to reiterate here is that religious fundamentalism has not been the immediate, spontaneous and natural choice of the Arabs or of Muslims in general.

They were not tempted to go along that path until all others were blocked. And until, paradoxically, that path itself — the path of atavism and conservatism — had come back into fashion and was "in the air" again.

3

The Age of Global Tribes

1

OF COURSE "IN THE AIR" is not a very rigorous expression. I use it to suggest the diffuse and elusive phenomenon that at certain moments in history makes a lot of people start to emphasise one element of their identity rather than the rest. Thus, at present, it is common for a person to stress his or her religious allegiance and regard it as the central factor in his or her identity. This attitude is probably less widespread now than it was 300 years ago, but it is undoubtedly more general than it was 50 years ago.

I could have spoken of intellectual environment or emotional climate — both of them terms scarcely less vague than "in the air." But whatever expressions one decides to employ, it's the real questions underlying them that matter: what is it that currently makes men and women all over the world, from every kind of background, rediscover and feel impelled to assert in various ways their religious affiliation, when the same people, only a few years earlier, would spontaneously have chosen to put forward quite different allegiances? What makes a Muslim in Yugoslavia suddenly stop calling himself a Yugoslav and proclaim himself first and foremost a Muslim? What causes a Jewish worker in Russia who all his life has regarded himself as a proletarian, suddenly begin to see himself as a Jew? How does it happen that the proud affirmation of subscribing to some religion, which might once have appeared unseemly, now strikes people in so many countries at the same time as quite natural and permissible?

It is a complex phenomenon with no single satisfactory explanation. Nonetheless, it is clear that a decisive role was played in its development by the decline, followed by the collapse, of the communist world. It is more than a century since Marxism promised to establish a new worldwide society from which the notion of God would be banished. The failure of this project not only on the economic and political, but also on the moral and intellectual planes, has resulted in the rehabilitation of beliefs that Marxism itself wanted to consign to the dustbins of history. From Poland to Afghanistan, religion, that spiritual refuge and buttress of identity, was an obvious rallying point for all who were fighting communism. So the defeat of Marx and Lenin has been perceived as the revenge of religions at least as much as the victory of capitalism, liberalism and the West.

But this is not the only operative factor behind the "rise" of religion in the last quarter of the twentieth century. While the terminal crisis of communism has weighed heavily on intellectual and political debate, and will continue to do so, many things would be incomprehensible if other factors were not taken into account, notably the other so-called "crisis" affecting the West.

This has to be considered as something quite different from the crisis of communism. It would be pointless to deny that in the long battle between the two sides there has been a winner and a loser. But nor can it be gainsaid that the western model, despite its triumph and the fact that its influence is spreading over every continent, sees itself as a model in crisis, unable to resolve the problems of poverty in its own cities, incapable of attacking unemployment, delinquency, drugs and many other scourges. It is one of our age's most disconcerting paradoxes that the most attractive model of society, the one that has overcome all the others, has deeply-felt doubts about itself.

Let us for a moment put ourselves in the place of a young man of 19 who has just entered a university in the Arab world. In the past he might have been attracted by an organisation with Marxist tendencies that would have been sympathetic to his existential difficulties and initiated him, in its own way, into the debate about ideas. Or else he might have joined some nationalist group that would have flattered his need for identity and perhaps spoken to him of renaissance and modernisation. But now Marxism has lost its attraction and Arab nationalism, annexed by regimes that are authoritarian, incompetent and corrupt, has lost much of its credibility. So it is not impossible that the young man we are thinking of will be fascinated by the West, by its way of life and its scientific and technological achievements. But that fascination would probably have little impact on his actions, since there is no political organisation of any consequence that embodies the model he admires. Those who aspire to the "Western Paradise" often have no alternative but emigration.

Unless they belong to one of the privileged "castes" who do their best to reproduce aspects of the coveted model in their own homes. But all those who are not born with a limousine at their disposal, all those who want to shake up the established order or are revolted by corruption, state despotism, inequality, unemployment and lack of opportunity, all who have difficulty finding a place in a fast-changing world — all these are tempted by Islamism. In it they find satisfaction for their need for identity, for affiliation to a group, for spirituality, for a simple interpretation of too-complex realities and for action and revolt.

I can't help feeling deeply uneasy as I point out the circumstances that lead young people in the Muslim world to enrol in religious movements. This is because, in the conflict between the Islamists and the rulers who oppose them, I find myself unable to identify with either side. I am unmoved by the utterances of radical Islamists not only because as a Christian I feel excluded, but also because I cannot accept that any religious faction, even if it is in the majority, has the right to lay down the law for the population as a whole. In my view the tyranny of a majority is no better morally than the tyranny of a minority. Moreover, I believe profoundly not just in equality, between men and women alike, but also in liberty in matters of faith and in the freedom of every individual to live as he chooses; and I distrust any doctrine that tries to challenge such fundamental values.

That said, I must add that I disapprove just as strongly of the despotic powers against which the Islamists are fighting, and I decline to applaud the outrages such regimes perpetrate on the pretext that they constitute a lesser evil. The people themselves deserve something better than a lesser evil or any sort of makeshift. What they need are genuine solutions, which can only be those of genuine democracy and modernity — by which I mean a complete modernity freely granted, not an eviscerated one imposed by force. And it seems to me that by taking a fresh look at the idea of identity we might help find a way that leads out of the present impasse and towards human liberty.

I now end this digression and return to what is "in the air." And also to say that if the rise of the religious factor can be explained partly by the discomfiture of communism, partly by the impasse in which various Third World societies find themselves, and partly by the crisis affecting the western model, the scope and tone of the phenomenon cannot be understood except with reference, in particular, to the spectacular progress made recently in the field of communications and, in general, to what is usually called globalisation.

In a text published in 1973, the British historian Arnold Toynbee explained that the history of the human race had consisted of three successive phases.

During the first, which corresponds to prehistory, communications were extremely slow, but knowledge advanced even more painfully, so that every new development had time to spread everywhere before another came along. Thus all human societies evolved roughly in parallel with one another and had many characteristics in common.

In the second period, knowledge developed at a much faster rate than the means of disseminating it, so that in every field human societies grew more and more different from one another. This phase lasted for several thousand years, which corresponds to what we call History.

Then, quite recently, a third period has begun, in which although knowledge certainly advances more and more rapidly, the dissemination of knowledge progresses even faster, with the result that human societies are likely to become less and less differentiated from one another.

We could spend some time discussing the validity of this theory, which I have in any case presented in very simplified terms. However, I put it forward not as a basis for argument but rather as an appealing and intellectually stimulating insight into the situation we see around us today.

It is obvious that the current universal, ever more intense and apparently uncontrollable interchange of images and ideas will bring about a profound and, in terms of the history of civilisation, very swift transformation in our knowledge, perceptions and behaviour. Moreover, it will probably have an equally fundamental effect on our vision of ourselves, our allegiances and our identity. Extrapolating Toynbee's hypothesis slightly, we might say that everything human societies have done through the ages to mark differences and establish frontiers between them is due to come under pressures aimed at reducing those differences and abolishing those frontiers.

But the unprecedented metamorphosis taking place before our very eyes, like some endless but ever-accelerating fireworks display, brings with it certain shocks. We all accept many things offered by the world around us just because they seem either advantageous or inevitable. But each one of us has known what it is to jib when he feels that some significant factor in his identity is being threatened, whether it be his language, his religion, the symbolic elements in his culture, or his independence. So we are living in an age of both harmonisation and dissonance. Never have men had so many things in common — knowledge, points of reference, images, words, instruments and tools of all kinds. But this only increases their desire to assert their differences.

All this is plain to the naked eye. The ever-increasing speed of globalisation undoubtedly reinforces, by way of reaction, people's need for identity. And because of the existential anguish that accompanies such sudden changes it also strengthens their need for spirituality. But only religious allegiance meets, or at least seeks to meet, both these needs.

I have mentioned the word "reaction," but I should point out that it alone cannot account for the phenomenon as a whole. True, we may call it reaction, in every sense of the word, when a group of people, frightened by change, seeks refuge in the values and symbols of a time-honoured tradition. But it seems to me that there is something more than mere reaction in the current rise of religious sentiment: perhaps an attempt at a synthesis between the need for identity and the desire for universality. I see the religious communities as global tribes: tribes because of their stress on identity, global because of the way they blithely reach across frontiers. For some people, to subscribe to a faith that transcends national, regional and social affiliations is a way of proclaiming their own universality. In a way, belonging to a faith community is the most global and universal kind of particularism — or perhaps rather the most tangible, the most "natural," the most deep-rooted.

Whatever the right term for it may be, the important thing is to note that, as it manifests itself today, the feeling of belonging to a religious community is not merely a return to the past. We are witnessing not the dawn, but the twilight of the age of nationalities. We are also living through not the dawn but the dusk of internationalism too, at least in its "proletarian" form. So the sense of belonging first and foremost to a religion cannot just be brushed aside as a fleeting historical moment, soon to be left behind. For the question has to be asked: left behind for what? For a new era of nations? That seems to me neither likely nor even desirable. In any case, the sense of belonging to a common "Church" is nowadays the most efficient factor for binding together varieties of nationalism, even those that call themselves secular. This is as true of the Turks as of the Russians, Greeks, Poles and Israelis, and for many other groups who wouldn't care to admit it.

So what will religious affiliation be replaced by? What other allegiance will be able to make it "obsolete," as it once seemed to be before?

2

A T THIS STAGE OF MY ARGUMENT a clarification is necessary if I am to avoid serious misunderstanding. When I speak of leaving religious allegiance behind I am not trying to say that religion itself should become a thing of the past. For me, religion will never be consigned to the storeroom of history either by science, by doctrine of some other kind or by any political regime. The further science progresses the more man is bound to ponder the purpose of his own existence. The God of "how" will become hazy one day, but the God of "why" will never die. Perhaps a thousand years hence we won't have the same religions as now, but I can't imagine the world without any kind of religion at all.

I hasten to add that in my view the need for spirituality doesn't have to express itself through participation in a religious community. We are concerned here with two fundamental aspirations, both of which are in differing degrees natural and permissible, but which we must be careful to distinguish. On the one hand there is the desire for a vision of the world that transcends our own existence with its sufferings and disappointments, and gives a meaning — even if only an illusory one — to life and death. On the other hand there is the need, felt by every individual, to feel part of a community which accepts and recognises him and within which he can be understood easily.

I dream not of a world where religion no longer has any place but of one where the need for spirituality will no longer be associated with the need to belong. A world in which a man, while remaining attached to his beliefs, to a faith, or to moral values that may or may not be inspired by scripture, will no longer feel the need to enrol himself among his co-religionists. A world in which religion will no longer serve to bind together warring ethnic groups. It is not enough now to separate Church and State: what has to do with religion must be kept apart from what has to do with identity. And if we want that amalgam to stop feeding fanaticism, terror and ethnic wars, we must find other ways of satisfying the need for identity.

This brings me back to my original question: what can be done today to replace affiliation to a religious community?

The difficulty, as suggested in the previous pages, is that such an affiliation seems now to be the ultimate allegiance, the least ephemeral, the most deep-rooted, the only one capable of fulfilling so many of man's essential needs. It also looks as if it cannot be permanently supplanted by other traditional allegiances, whether to nation, ethnic group, race or even class; these all turn out to be narrower, more restrictive and scarcely less lethal. If affiliation to a "global tribe" is to be left behind, it can only be for a much wider allegiance, with a fuller vision of humanity.

Of course, you say. But which? What "wider allegiance"? What "vision of humanity"? A glance round the world is enough to show that there is no new affiliation capable of counterbalancing the powerful visceral allegiances that have demonstrated throughout the course of history their ability to arouse armies of followers. Moreover, any would-be global vision provokes mistrust among our contemporaries, either because it strikes them as naive or because it seems to threaten their identity.

Mistrust is undoubtedly one of the keywords of our age. Mistrust of ideologies, of dreams of a better future, of politics, science, reason and modernity. Of the idea of progress. Of practically everything we could believe in throughout the twentieth century — a century of great achievements, without any precedent ever, but also a century of unforgivable crimes and blighted hopes. Mistrust, too, of anything that presents itself as global, worldwide or planetary.

Only a few years ago many people would have been ready to see the idea of a worldwide allegiance as being in some way the natural culmination of human history. Thus an inhabitant of Turin, having been first a Piedmontese and then an Italian, would become next a European and thereafter a citizen of the world. I am simplifying greatly, but the notion of an irreversible progress towards ever-wider affiliations did not seem far-fetched then. Through a series of regional regroupings the human race itself would ultimately become the supreme group. There were even very attractive theories concerning the two rival systems, the capitalist and the communist, which would gradually converge, the former becoming ever more social, the latter ever less interventionist, until they finally fused into one. Similarly it was predicted that religions would eventually all come together in one great cosy syncretism.

We know now that history never follows the path we predict. This is not because history is by nature erratic, unfathomable or indecipherable, or because human reason cannot comprehend it. It is precisely because history is not just what men make of it but rather the sum of all their individual and collective acts, all their words, communications, confrontations, sufferings, hatreds and affinities. The more numerous and free the humans who make history, the more complex and difficult to understand is the total result of all their actions, and the less amenable to simplistic explanations.

History is continually advancing along an infinite number of paths. Does some meaning nevertheless emerge? Until we reach "The End" — if *that* means anything — we shall probably never know.

Will the future be that of our hopes or that of our nightmares? Will it consist of freedom or slavery? Will science ultimately be the means of our redemption or the instrument of our destruction? Will we have been the inspired assistants of a Creator or no more than mere sorcerers' apprentices? Are we moving towards a better world or towards "the best of all possible worlds"?

And, to begin with, what do the coming decades have in store for us? A "war of civilisations" or the peace of the "global village"?

I firmly believe that the future is not written down anywhere. The future will be what we make it.

"But what about fate?" some will ask, alluding to the fact that I'm an oriental. My usual reply is that fate is to man as the wind is to a sailing boat. The helmsman cannot decide the direction or the force of the wind, but he can manipulate his own sails. And that can make an enormous difference. The same wind that may kill a mariner who is inexperienced, rash or merely unlucky will bring another safe to harbour.

Almost the same can be said of the "wind" of globalisation that is now sweeping the world. It would be absurd to try to stop it, but if we navigate skilfully, steering a steady course and avoiding reefs, we can reach haven safe and sound.

But the marine metaphor is too limited. I want to express myself more clearly. There is no point in asking ourselves whether the great technological progress that has been accelerating in recent years and that has profoundly changed our lives, especially in the field of communications and access to knowledge, is a good thing or a bad thing as far as we are concerned. It isn't the subject of a referendum. It's a fact. But the way it affects our future depends largely upon ourselves.

Some people might be tempted to reject it all out of hand, taking refuge in their "identity" and anathematising in one and the same breath globalisation, the hegemony of the West and the intolerable United States. Others, conversely, would be ready to accept everything, to swallow it all so indiscriminately that they end up not knowing where they are, where they are going or what the world is coming to! The two attitudes are diametrically opposite, but both end up in resignation. Both of them — the bitter and the cloying, the surly and the silly — are based on the premise that the world moves forward like a train on its rails and that nothing can make it alter its course.

I think differently. It seems to me that the wind of globalisation, while it certainly could lead us to disaster, could also lead us to success. While the new means of communication that all too swiftly bring us close to one another may bring us by way of reaction to stress our differences, they also make us aware of our common fate. This makes me think that current developments might in the long run favour the emergence of a new approach to the idea of identity. Identity would then be seen as the sum of all our allegiances, and, within it, allegiance to the human community itself would become increasingly important, until one day it would become the chief allegiance, though without destroying our many individual affiliations. Of course I wouldn't go as far as to say that the wind of globalisation *must* blow us in that direction, but it seems to me it makes such an attitude less difficult to imagine. And, at the same time, necessary.

3

"MEN ARE MORE THE SONS OF THEIR TIME than of their fathers," wrote the historian Marc Bloch. The maxim has probably always been true, but never more so than now. There is no need to insist further on how, in the last few decades, things have been moving ever faster. Which of our contemporaries has not sometimes felt he has witnessed in a couple of years changes that in the past would have been spread over a century? The oldest among us even have to make an effort to recall what their outlook was like in their childhood, and to do so they have to set aside the habits they have acquired since, together with new products and tools they cannot now do without. As for the young, they often haven't the slightest idea what their grandparents' way of life was like, let alone that of earlier generations.

In fact, we are all infinitely closer to our contemporaries than to our ancestors. Would it be an exaggeration to say I have much more in common with a random passerby in a street in Prague or Seoul or San Francisco than with my own great-grandfather? And this not only as regards appearance, clothes, behaviour, way of life, work, habitat and the objects that surround us, but also as regards moral concepts and habits of thought.

The same applies to belief. We may call ourselves Christians — or Muslims, Jews, Buddhists or Hindus — but our vision of both this world and the next no longer bears much resemblance to that of our "co-religionists" who lived 500 years ago. For the great majority of them, Hell was as real a place as Asia Minor or Abyssinia, complete with cloven-hoofed devils thrusting sinners into eternal fire, as in apocalyptic paintings. Practically no one thinks like that now. The example I chose was extreme, but the observation itself applies equally well to all our ideas in every field. Many types of behaviour that are perfectly acceptable to a believer today would have struck his "co-religionists" in the past as inconceivable. I put the word in quotes because the religion practised by our ancestors was not the same as ours. If we had lived among them and behaved as we do nowadays we would have been stoned in the street, thrown into prison or burned at the stake for impiety, debauchery, heresy or witchcraft.

In short, each one of us has two heritages, a "vertical" one that comes to us from our ancestors, our religious community and our popular traditions, and a "horizontal" one transmitted to us by our contemporaries and by the age we live in. It seems to me that the latter is the more influential of the two, and that it becomes more so every day. Yet this fact is not reflected in our perception of ourselves, and the inheritance we invoke most frequently is the vertical one.

This is an essential point with regard to current concepts of identity. On the one hand there is what we are in reality and what we are becoming as a result of cultural globalisation: that is to say, beings woven out of many-coloured threads, who share most of their points of reference, their ways of behaving and their beliefs with the vast community of their contemporaries. And on the other hand there is what we think we are and what we claim to be: that is to say, members of one community rather than another, adherents of one faith rather than another. I do not deny the importance of our religious, national or other affiliations. I do not question the often decisive influence of our vertical heritage. But it is necessary at this point in time to draw attention to the gulf that exists between what we are and what we think we are.

To tell the truth, if we assert our differences so fiercely it is precisely because we are less and less different from one another. Because, in spite of our conflicts and our age-old enmities, each day that goes by reduces our differences and increases our likenesses a little bit more.

I seem to be glad of this. But should one rejoice to see people growing more and more like one another? Are we heading for an insipid world where we may soon speak only one language, where everyone shares the same bunch of minimal beliefs, and where everyone watches the same American TV soaps, munching the same sandwiches?

Caricature aside, the question needs to be seriously addressed. We are living in a very bewildering age, in which many of our fellow-creatures see globalisation not as a great and enriching amalgam with advantages for all, but as a standardisation and an impoverishment, a threat that the individual needs to fight against in order to preserve his own culture, identity and values.

These may be merely rear-guard actions, but in present circumstances we must have the humility to admit we don't really know. We may not always find what we expect in the dustbins of history. In any case, if so many people see globalisation as a threat it is only natural that we should examine it more closely.

Those who feel themselves to be in danger may of course be influenced in part by the fear of change that is as old as mankind itself. But there are other, more current anxieties which I'd hesitate to dismiss as irrelevant. For globalisation draws us simultaneously towards two contrasting results, one welcome and the other not: i.e., universality and uniformity. The two tracks seem so alike and are so closely intermingled it's as if there were only one. You might almost wonder if one isn't just the presentable face of the other.

But for my part I'm sure there are two separate tracks, however much and however closely they intertwine. It would be over-optimistic to try to unravel the whole skein at once, but we might well attempt to tease out a thread or two.

4

THE BASIC POSTULATE OF UNIVERSALITY IS that there exist inherent rights to human dignity that no one may deny to his fellow creatures, whether on the grounds of religion, colour, nationality or sex, or on any other consideration. This means, among other things, that any attack on the fundamental rights of men and women in the name of some tradition — religious or other — is contrary to the spirit of universality. There cannot be on the one hand an overall, general charter of human rights and on the other hand special and particular charters for Muslims, Jews, Christians, Africans, Asians and the rest.

Few people would disagree with this in principle. But in practice many behave as if they didn't really believe it. For example, no western government scrutinises human rights in Africa or the Arab world as closely as it does in Poland or Cuba. This attitude claims to be motivated by respect, but in my view it is really based on contempt. If you respect someone and respect his history it's because you believe he belongs to the same human race as you do, not to some inferior version.

I don't wish to dwell on this question, which calls for lengthy argument in its own right. But I refer to it in passing because it plays an essential part in the notion of universality, which would be meaningless if it didn't presuppose that there are values that concern the whole human race without exception. And these values come before all else. Traditions deserve to be respected only insofar as they are respectable — that is, exactly insofar as they themselves respect the fundamental rights of men and women. To follow traditions or to obey laws that are discriminatory is to despise their victims. Every country and every doctrine has at certain times in its history produced behaviour which, with the evolution of mental attitudes, has come to be regarded as incompatible with human dignity. Such practices cannot be wiped out by a stroke of the pen, but that doesn't exempt us from denouncing them and doing our best to make them things of the past.

Everything that has to do with fundamental rights — the right to live as a full citizen on the soil of one's fathers, free of persecution or discrimination; the right to live with dignity anywhere; the right to choose one's life and loves and beliefs freely, while respecting the freedom of others; the right of free access to knowledge, health and a decent and honourable life — none of this, and the list is not exhaustive, may be denied to our fellow human beings on the pretext of preserving a belief, an ancestral practice or a tradition. In this area we should tend towards universality, and even, if necessary, towards uniformity, because humanity, while it is also multiple, is primarily one.

What then about the individuality of each civilisation? Of course it has to be respected, but differently and with lucidity.

At the same time as we fight for the universality of values it is imperative that we fight against the impoverishment of standardisation; against hegemony, whether ideological, political, economic or operating in the media; against foolish conformism; against everything that stifles the full variety of linguistic, artistic and intellectual expression. Against everything that makes for a monotonous and puerile world. A battle in defence of certain practices and cultural traditions, but one that is clear-sighted, rigorous, discriminating, not oversensitive, not unduly timorous, always open to the future.

A great tide of different images, sounds, ideas and products submerges the whole planet, bringing every day new changes to our tastes, hopes, habits, life style and view of the world, and also to ourselves. This extraordinary ferment often brings forth contradictions. For example, we now see the familiar American fast food signs on the main streets of Paris, Moscow, Shanghai and Prague. But it is also true that on every continent we encounter more and more different kinds of cooking, not only Italian, French, Chinese and Indian, which have been exported for a long time now, but also Japanese, Indonesian, Korean, Mexican, Moroccan and Lebanese.

For some people that is a mere detail. But for me it is very revealing. It shows what the great mingling of cultures may mean in terms of everyday life. It also reflects people's different reactions. Many see this phenomenon merely as proof of some young people's fascination with American ways. I am not in favour of laisser-faire, and I admire those who stand up for themselves. It's permissible and sometimes necessary to fight to preserve the traditional character of a street, a neighbourhood, or a certain quality of life. But that shouldn't prevent us from seeing the picture as a whole.

That fact that all over the world you can now eat not only the local food but also, if you choose, try out other culinary traditions, not excluding those of the United States; the fact that the British might like mint sauce with their curry, that the French sometimes order a couscous instead of a stew, or that an inhabitant of Minsk, after decades of dullness, fancies a hamburger with ketchup — none of this irritates or bothers me. On the contrary, I'd like every culinary tradition to be enjoyed all over the world, whether it comes from Szechuan, Aleppo, Champagne, Apulia, Hanover or Milwaukee.

What I have said of cuisine could be extended to many other aspects of everyday culture. Music, for example. Here again, an extraordinary proliferation is taking place. The news from Algeria is often appalling, but from the same country there also emanates inventive music of many kinds, disseminated by young people who express themselves in Arabic, French or Kabyle. Some of them have stayed at home, despite everything, while others have gone abroad, taking with them, in them, and bearing witness to, the truth of a people and the soul of a culture.

Their journey cannot fail to remind us of the older, more massive trajectory of the Africans once taken as slaves to the Americas. Today their music, whether issuing from Louisiana or from the West Indies, has spread all over the world and become part of the musical and emotional heritage of us all. That is globalisation too. Never in the past have human beings had the technical means of listening at will to so many kinds of music — all those voices, whether from Cameroon, Spain, Egypt, Argentina, Brazil and Cape Verde, or from Liverpool, Memphis, Brussels and Naples. Never before have so many people been able to play, compose, sing — and be heard.

5

THOUGH I STRESS WHAT SEEMS TO ME to be one of the advantages of globalisation, a genuine example of universality, I don't wish to ignore the unease of those who see the present upsurge of new music as much less significant than the growing predominance of English-speaking influence in popular song. This anxiety exists in many other fields — in some sectors of the international media, for instance, and in the cinema, where the influence of Hollywood is clearly overwhelming.

I've spoken of unease, but that is too vague a word to encompass the wide range of reactions involved. A French café owner annoyed at hearing so few French songs on the radio has nothing in common — except perhaps mistrust of global culture in its present form — with a fanatical preacher who calls satellite dishes satanic dishes because he regards them as transmitters of the siren voices of the West. Personally, I am worried, simultaneously but not equally, by both anxieties. I don't want the Arab world to look backwards and rage against modernity; but nor do I want France to enter the new millennium hesitant and unsure of herself.

But as I've said before, although the worries people have about globalisation sometimes strike me as excessive, I don't consider them unfounded.

They are of two kinds. I shall refer to the first kind more briefly than it deserves, because treating it fully would call for more space than is available here. It consists of the idea that the present ferment, rather than leading to a great enrichment, a multiplication of the means of expression and the diversification of opinion, instead conduces to the opposite — to impoverishment. According to this point of view, the current free outpouring of musical expression will ultimately result in no more than sugary, mawkish "wallpaper," and the extraordinary effervescence of ideas will produce only a simplistic conformism, an intellectual lowest common denominator. So much so that everyone, with the exception of a few eccentrics, will soon end up reading (if they read anything at all) the same stereotyped novels, listening to the same vague mass-produced tunes, and watching films all made according to the same recipes — in short, swallowing the same formless pap of sounds, images and beliefs.

The prospect facing the news media might be considered equally frustrating. Sometimes it's thought that with so many newspapers and radio and television channels likely to be available we shall have access to an infinite variety of opinions. Then the reverse seems to be true: the transmitters are so powerful that they merely amplify the currently prevailing opinion, drowning out any other point of view. And admittedly, the flood of words and images doesn't always encourage a spirit of criticism.

Are we then to conclude that a ferment such as we are witnessing at present, instead of favouring cultural diversity really leads, by virtue of some insidious law, to uniformity? The risk undoubtedly exists: we catch a glimpse of it in the tyranny of ratings and the excesses of political correctness. But it's a risk inherent in any democratic system. And though we may fear the worst if we were to rely passively on the power of numbers, disaster is not inevitable if we make good use of the means of expression at our disposal and are able to see through the simplistic reality of figures to the complex reality of human beings.

For it need hardly be said that, despite certain appearances, we live not in the age of the masses but in that of the individual. From this point of view, humanity, having skirted some of the worst dangers in its history during the course of the twentieth century, has emerged rather better than was expected.

Although world population has almost quadrupled in a hundred years it seems to me that on the whole everyone is now more conscious than in the past of his individuality, more aware of his rights, if probably slightly less so of his duties, and more concerned with his place in society, his health, his well-being, his body, his personal future, the powers at his disposal, and his identity — however he may interpret this notion. I also think that each one of us, if he can learn to make use of the unprecedented tools now within his reach, can exercise a significant influence both on his contemporaries and on future generations. On condition that he has something to say to them. On condition too that he is

THE AGE OF GLOBAL TRIBES

inventive, for the new realities don't come to us with instructions attached.

Above all, on condition that he doesn't cringe at home, abjuring the cruel world.

Such timidity would be equally fruitless with regard to the second anxiety aroused by globalisation: standardisation not through mediocrity but through hegemony. This worry is more widespread and is the source not only of countless tensions but also of many bloody conflicts.

It may be expressed as follows: is globalisation just another word for Americanisation? Won't its main result be to impose on the whole world one language; one economic, political and social system; one way of life; one scale of values — those of the United States of America? According to some people, the whole phenomenon of globalisation is nothing but a masquerade, a camouflage, a Trojan horse concealing an attempt at domination.

But for a rational observer it is absurd to suppose that technological progress and moral evolution might be wholly subject to a remote control exercised by one great power or a coalition of great powers. On the other hand, we might well ask ourselves whether globalisation will not at least favour the predominance of one civilisation or the hegemony of one power. That would entail two serious dangers, the first being the gradual disappearance of some languages, traditions and cultures, and the second being the adoption by cultures that are threatened of increasingly radical or suicidal attitudes.

The risks of hegemony are real. It is even euphemistic to speak of mere risks. There can be no doubt that over the centuries Western civilisation has acquired a privileged status vis-à-vis the others — those of Asia, Africa, pre-Colombian America and Eastern Europe — which have become increasingly marginalised and profoundly influenced, not to say remodelled, by the Christian West. Nor can it be denied that with the collapse of the Soviet Union the Western developed countries have managed to establish the absolute preeminence of their own economic and political system, which is in the process of becoming the norm for the whole world.

Similarly, it is superfluous to cite examples of how, since the end of the cold war, the United States, now the only genuine superpower, has come to exercise unprecedented influence over the entire planet. This influence manifests itself in a variety of ways: sometimes through deliberate action, to settle some regional conflict, to destabilise an enemy or to subvert a rival's economic policy; but sometimes also involuntarily, through the force and attraction of the model it offers. Millions of men and women from every other kind of culture are tempted to imitate the Americans — to eat or dress, to speak or sing as they do, or as they are supposed to do.

It seems to me worth recalling these facts before posing the questions that arise from them. For example, to what extent is the global culture, as it develops daily, essentially Western or even specifically American? From that question others follow. What is going to become of all the other cultures? What will happen to all the different languages we speak today? Will they just be reduced to local dialects, doomed sooner or later to disappear? And what will be the atmosphere in which globalisation takes place in coming decades, if it emerges as more and more destructive not only of cultures, languages, rituals, beliefs and traditions, but also of identities? If all of us were asked to deny our own selves in order to attain modernity as it is defined now and will be defined in future, would not conservatism and atavism, not to mention violence, be an increasingly general reaction?

4

Taming the Panther

1

NEITHER IN THE PRECEDING PAGES nor in those that follow does this book try to cover all the phenomena — economic, technological, geopolitical and so on — involved in the notion of globalisation. Nor have my previous chapters aimed at dealing exhaustively with the vast subject of identity. From this point on too, my objective is much more modest and precise. I want to try to understand how globalisation exacerbates behaviour as it relates to identity, but how one day it might make that behaviour less lethal.

I start out from the observation that whenever a society sees "the hand of the stranger" in modernity it tends to repulse it and try to ward it off. I've spoken at length of the Arab-Muslim world and its complicated relationships with all that comes to it from the West. A similar state of affairs can be seen today in various parts of the world with regard to globalisation. And if we want to avoid seeing the latter unleash in millions upon millions of our fellow human beings a reaction of furious, suicidal, systematic rejection, it is essential that the global civilisation which globalisation in general is creating should not seem to be exclusively American. Everyone must be able to recognise himself in it, to identify with it a little. No one must be made to think it is irremediably alien and therefore hostile to him.

Here again the key principle is reciprocity. Nowadays we all have to incorporate into our lives countless ingredients that come to us from the most powerful of the world's cultures. But it is vital that we should all be able to see that elements of our own culture — individuals who have distinguished themselves, fashions, works of art, everyday objects, music, food, words — are also adopted all over the world, including North America, and form part of the universal heritage of all mankind.

Identity is in the first place a matter of symbols, even of appearances. When, in any gathering, I see people with names that sound like mine, with the same colour skin, with the same affinities, even the same infirmities, it is possible for me to feel that that gathering represents me. A "thread of affiliation" links me to the crowd: the thread may be thick or thin, strong or weak, but it is easily recognisable by all those who are sensitive on the subject of identity.

What is true of a gathering is just as true of a social group, a national community, and the global community itself. Wherever you are you need these signs of identification, these bridges to the Other: this is still the most "civil" way of satisfying the need for identity.

Some societies are careful about this aspect of things when it's a matter of reducing their own internal tensions, but are much less so when it comes to the relations between different cultures in a worldwide context. I am thinking, of course, of the United States. There, whether your origins are Polish, Irish, Italian, African or Hispanic, whenever you sit down in front of your television set you inevitably see a procession of names and faces that are Polish, Irish, Italian, African or Hispanic. Sometimes this is so systematic, so fabricated and conventional that it is irritating. Nine times out of ten the rapist in a police series has fair hair and blue eyes, so as to avoid giving a negative impression of any minorities. And if the delinquent is black and the detective pursuing him is white, the police chief has to be black too. Annoying? Perhaps. But when you remember the old cowboy and Indian films and the wild applause with which kids used to greet the scenes where the Indians were mown down wholesale, you're inclined to conclude that the present attitude is a lesser evil.

But I don't want to give such balancing acts more credit than they deserve. Though they may sometimes help to damp down racial, ethnic or other prejudices, they often help to perpetuate them. In the name of the same principle — "that no American should be offended by what he sees or hears" — there used to be a virtual ban on showing any marriage or other union between a white man and a black woman or a white woman and a black man, because public opinion, we are told, doesn't feel comfortable with mixed relationships of that kind. So everyone has to "go around" only with members of his or her own "tribe." Here again the manoeuvres are so systematic and predictable that the result is exasperating, even insulting.

Such are the more childish excesses of would-be collectivism. But in my view they do not detract from the rightness of the simple idea prevailing in the United States today, according to which every citizen, especially every member of a minority, should encounter recognisable names and faces when he watches television, and should see himself represented positively to prevent him from feeling excluded from the national community.

The idea deserves to be adopted on a wider scale. Since people all over the world now have access to the same images, sounds and products, wouldn't it be more appropriate if all those images, sounds and products were representative of all cultures, so that everyone could recognise himself in them and no one feel excluded? Neither on a world scale nor within any society should anybody feel so scorned, depreciated, mocked or demonised that in order to be able to live among his fellow-citizens he is forced to conceal or be ashamed of his religion, colour, language, name or any other ingredient of his identity. Everyone ought to be able to hold his head high and acknowledge without fear or resentment every one of his allegiances.

It would be disastrous if the current globalisation were to be a one-way process, with "universal transmitters" on one side and "receivers" on the other, with the "norm" set against the "exceptions"; with on the one hand those who think they have nothing to learn from the rest of the world, and on the other those who believe that the rest of the world will never listen to them.

I am thinking here not only of the danger of hegemony but also of its converse or negative image — the equally grave danger of pique and resentment that may be observed in various parts of the world.

Many are so angry or bewildered that they give up trying to understand what is going on. Many refuse to make a contribution to the emerging universal culture because at some point they decided once and for all that the world around them was incomprehensible, hostile, bloodthirsty, demented or diabolical. Many are tempted to see themselves as mere victims — victims of America, of the West, of capitalism or liberalism, of the new technologies, of the media, of change, and so on. It cannot be denied that such people really do feel wronged and suffer accordingly, but their reaction seems to me inappropriate. To imprison oneself in a victim mentality can do the injured party even more harm than the aggression itself. And this is as true of societies as of individuals. They huddle themselves away, they barricade themselves in, they try to ward off everything, they close their minds, they ruminate, they give up looking for anything new, they don't explore anymore, they don't make any more progress, they are afraid of the future, of the present and of everyone else.

To those who react in this way I always feel like saying: the world of today isn't really how you imagine it! It's not true that it's ruled by dark and omnipotent forces. It's not true that it belongs to the "others." No doubt the scale on which globalisation is taking place, together with the dizzying speed of change, make all of us feel as if we're being submerged by it all and unable to affect the course of events. But we must keep reminding ourselves that this feeling is extremely widespread, and shared even by those we tend to think of as safely ensconced on the top of the heap.

In an earlier chapter I said that everyone nowadays felt himself to be living to a certain extent in a minority, in exile. This is because all communities and cultures have a sense that they are up against others stronger than they, a feeling that they can no longer keep their heritage safe. Looked at from the South and the East, it is the West that dominates. Looked at from Paris, it is America that holds sway. But if you go to the United States, then what do you see? You see minorities reflecting all the diversity in the world, all needing to assert their original allegiances. And when you have met all these minorities and been told a hundred times that power is in the hands of white males, or of Anglo-Saxon Protestants, you suddenly hear the sound of a huge explosion in Oklahoma City. And who are the people responsible? Some white male Anglo-Saxon Protestants who regard themselves as members of the most neglected and despised of minorities, and who believe that globalisation is sounding the knell of "their" America. In the eyes of everyone else, Timothy McVeigh and his supporters belong to the same ethnic group as those who are supposed to dominate the planet and hold our future in their hands. In their own eyes they are merely an endangered species, with no other weapon available to them but the most murderous terrorism.

So who does the world really belong to? Not to any particular race or any particular country. More than at any other time in history it belongs to all those who want to make a place for themselves in it. It belongs to all those who endeavour to understand the new rules of the game, however bewildering they may be, and try to use them to their own advantage.

Let there be no mistake: I am not trying to draw a veil over the horrors and ugliness of the world we live in. Throughout this book I have continually denounced its dysfunctions, its extremes, its inequalities and its excesses. But what I am passionately concerned to do is to counter the temptation to despair, to oppose the tendency, widespread among members of "peripheral" cultures, to sink into a permanent state of bitterness, resignation and passivity, from which they emerge only through suicidal violence.

I don't doubt that globalisation is a threat to cultural diversity, especially to diversity of languages and of lifestyles. I am even of the opinion that the danger is infinitely greater now than it was in the past, as I shall explain below. Nonetheless, the world of today also provides those who want to preserve endangered cultures with the means of self-defence. Instead of declining and disappearing unnoticed and unlamented as they have done for centuries, these cultures can now fight for survival. Would it not be absurd to neglect this opportunity?

The social and technological upheavals going on all around us constitute a historical phenomenon of great complexity and enormous scope, which everybody may take advantage of and nobody — not even America! — can control. Globalisation is not the tool of some "new order" that "some people" are trying to impose on the world. It is more like a huge arena, open on all sides, in which a thousand jousts and combats are taking place at the same time, making an indescribable and shattering din — an amphitheatre that anyone is free to enter with his own motto or theme song and with whatever banner or other paraphernalia he chooses.

The Internet, for example, seen from the outside and with a predisposition to mistrust, is an ectoplasmic monster enabling the powers that be to spread their tentacles over the whole planet. Seen from the inside, it is an extraordinary instrument of liberty, a reasonably egalitarian space which everyone can make use of as they wish and in which four bright students may wield as much influence as a head of state or an oil company. And although English is at present by far the dominant language here, more and more other languages make their mark on it every day thanks to some ingenious neologisms. Such inventions may still be hesitant, lame or even risible. Even so they bode well for the future.

More generally, the new means of communication offer very many of our contemporaries, people in every country, custodians of every cultural tradition, the opportunity to take part in the forging of a culture that will soon be common to us all.

If anyone wants to save his own language from dying out; if anyone wants to make the culture he grew up in known to and respected by the world as a whole; if anyone wants to see the community he belongs to attain freedom, democracy, dignity and well-being, the battle is not lost in advance. Examples from every continent show that those who fight skilfully against tyranny, obscurantism, segregation, contempt and neglect often win. As do those who fight against famine, ignorance and epidemics. We live in a wonderful age in which anyone with an idea, whether it be inspired, perverse or useless, can communicate it to millions of his fellow-men within 24 hours.

If you believe in something and have enough energy, passion and love of life, you can find among the resources offered by the world of today the means to make some of your dreams come true.

2

HAVE I, THROUGH THESE EXAMPLES, seemed to suggest that whenever the civilisation of today confronts us with a problem it providentially supplies us with the means of solving it? I don't think there are any grounds for such a generalisation. On the contrary, the formidable power lent to man by modern science and technology may be put to diametrically opposed uses, some beneficial and some destructive. Nature has never been so abused as it is today, yet we are in a much better position than ever before to protect it: not only because of our ability to influence environmental problems but also because our awareness of them is greater than in the past.

This does not mean our power to do good always gets the better of our ability to do harm, as is shown by all too many examples: take the depletion of the ozone layer, for instance, and the many species still threatened with extinction.

I might have referred to other fields besides that of the environment. I chose that because some of the dangers we encounter there are similar to those involved in globalisation.

In both cases there is a threat to diversity. Just as animal and plant species that have lived for millions of years are now dying out before our very eyes, in the same way, if we are not careful, we may witness the disappearance of many cultures that have hitherto managed to survive for hundreds or thousands of years.

Some are disappearing already. Certain languages stop being spoken before the last people to use them die themselves. Human communities that over the course of history have forged an original culture made up of a thousand and one inventions — relating to clothes, medicine, art, music, gestures, crafts, cooking, storytelling, and so on — are threatened with loss of their land, their language, their memory, their knowledge, their special identity and their dignity.

I'm not speaking only of small societies that have always lived outside the main trends of history, but also of countless other human communities in the East and West, North and South alike, all of which have their own characteristic features. It is not a question of freezing any of them at some particular point in their development, still less of changing them into a kind of sideshow. What we should aim at is preserving our common heritage of knowledge and activities in all its diversity and everywhere, from Provence to Borneo, from Louisiana to Amazonia; at giving all human beings the chance to live fully in the world of today, taking advantage of all its technical, social and intellectual advances without losing either their own particular collective memory or their dignity.

Why should we take the diversity of human cultures less seriously than the diversity of animal or plant species? Ought not our just desire to preserve our environment extend to the human environment itself? Our world would be a dreary place, both from the natural and from the cultural point of view, if the only surviving species were those we consider "useful," together with a few we judge to be decorative or that have acquired symbolic value.

When we consider all the various aspects of human culture it is clear we are dealing simultaneously with two quite different trends. Economics tends more and more to prize unbridled competition, whereas ecology is concerned with protection. The former is obviously part of the spirit of the age; but the latter will always have a right to be heard. Even the countries most in favour of untrammelled free trade pass laws aimed at, for example, preventing developers from damaging sites of natural interest. We sometimes need to take similar measures with regard to culture, to ring-fence threatened phenomena and prevent irreversible damage.

But that can only be a temporary solution. In the long term we ourselves, as citizens, need to step in. The battle for cultural diversity will only be won when we are as willing to engage our intellectual, emotional and practical forces in defence of an endangered language as we are to save the panda or the rhinoceros from extinction.

I keep mentioning language as one of the elements defining a culture or an identity, but I haven't stressed the fact that it is merely one of several equally significant factors. Now that the end of this book is in sight, perhaps it is time to spotlight language and give it its rightful importance.

Among all our recognised allegiances, this is almost always one of the most influential; almost as much so as religion, of which throughout history it has been in a way the main rival, though sometimes also its ally. When two communities speak different languages a common religion is not enough to unite them: take for instance the Catholic Flemings and Walloons, or the Turkish, Kurdish and Arab Muslims. Nor does a common language ensure that Orthodox Serbs, Catholic Croats and Muslims can coexist in Bosnia. All over the world, states constructed around a common language have been broken up by religious quarrels, while others, built around a common religion, have been torn to pieces by linguistic conflicts.

So much for rivalry. At the same time it is true that "alliances" lasting for centuries have been formed between Islam and the Arabic language, for example; between the Catholic Church and Latin; and between the Bible of Luther and the German language. If the Israelis are a nation today it is not only because of the religious links, powerful though they are, that bind them together, but also because they have managed to make modern Hebrew into a genuine national language. A person who lived in Israel for 40 years without ever going into a synagogue would not thereby exclude himself from the national community. The same could not be said of someone who lived there for 40 years without attempting to learn Hebrew. This is true of many other countries all over the world, and while it would not be difficult to prove that a man can live without a religion, clearly he cannot live without a language.

It is equally self-evident, though worth recalling in this context, that whereas religion tends by nature to be exclusive, language does not. A man can speak Hebrew, Arabic, Italian and Swedish, all at once, but he cannot be simultaneously a Jew, a Muslim, a Catholic and a Protestant. Even if someone regards himself as an adherent of two religions at once, such a position is not acceptable to other people.

I don't seek to express a preference between religion and language, or to prove that one is a greater determining factor than the other. I just want to draw attention to the fact that language has the marvellous characteristic of being both a component of identity and a means of communication. That being so, and contrary to my attitude in the case of religion, I regard any attempt to separate language from identity as neither possible nor desirable. Language is bound to remain the mainspring of cultural identity, and linguistic diversity the mainspring of all other diversities.

Without wishing to go into detail about so complex a phenomenon as the relationship between men and their languages, I think it is important, even within the limited scope of this book, to mention certain aspects of the question that specifically concern the notion of identity.

To begin with, every human being needs a language with which to identify and which is related to his sense of his own identity. That language may be common to hundreds of millions of individuals or just to a few thousand. Numbers are unimportant; what matters is the sense of belonging. Each one of us needs this powerful and reassuring link.

It is extremely dangerous to try to break the maternal cord connecting a man to his own language. When it is ruptured or seriously damaged his whole personality may suffer disastrous repercussions. The fanaticism that spills so much blood in Algeria is due even more to a language-linked frustration than to religion. France made little effort to convert the Muslims of Algeria to Christianity, but she did try to replace their language by her own, and she did so hastily and without bestowing real citizenship in exchange. I may say in passing that I have never understood how a country that called herself secular could call some of her citizens "French Muslims," and deprive them of some of their rights merely because they belonged to a religion other than her own.

To bring the digression to a close, this is only one of many tragic examples. I haven't the space to describe in detail all the disadvantages such people have to endure even today, and in all countries, just because they express themselves in a language that inspires mistrust, hostility, contempt and mockery in those about them.

It is essential that we establish clearly and without ambiguity, and that we watch over tirelessly, the right of every man to retain and to use freely the language which identifies him and with which he identifies. I regard that freedom as even more important than liberty of belief, which sometimes protects doctrines that themselves are hostile to liberty and contrary to the fundamental rights of women and men. I personally would have qualms about defending the right to free speech of those who advocate the abolition of freedoms and whose preachings incite hatred and tolerate slavery. I don't feel the slightest hesitation about proclaiming the right of every man to speak his own language.

Not that this right is always easy to put into effect. Even after the principle is asserted, the main task still remains to be done. Can everybody claim the right to go to a government office and speak the language of his own identity in the sure knowledge that the official behind the desk will understand him? Can a language that has long been oppressed, or at least neglected, legitimately claim its rightful place at the expense of others without provoking another kind of discrimination? Clearly I can't go into all the hundreds of different examples, from Pakistan to Quebec, from Nigeria to Catalonia. What we need to do is enter sensibly into an age of liberty and peaceful diversity, casting aside the injustices of the past without replacing them by new ones or by other kinds of exclusion or intolerance, and recognising the right of everyone to include several linguistic allegiances within his own identity.

Of course, all languages are not born equal. But I say of them what I say of people: they all possess an equal right to have their dignity respected. From the point of view of the need for identity, English and Icelandic play exactly the same role. It is only when we come to the other function of language, as a means of communication, that they cease to be equal.

3

I SHOULD LIKE TO DWELL FOR A FEW PAGES on the inequality between languages for a reason which touches me closely and to which I have already referred. In France, when I detect anxieties in some people about the way the world is going, or reservations about technological innovation, or some intellectual, verbal, musical or nutritional fashion; or when I see signs of oversensitivity, excessive nostalgia or even extreme attachment to the past — I realise that such reactions are often linked in one way or another to the resentment people feel about the continual advance of English and its present status as the predominant international language.

This attitude seems in some ways peculiar to France. Because France herself had global ambitions as regards language, she was the first to suffer on account of the extraordinary rise of English. For countries that had no such hopes, or had them no longer, the problem of relations with the predominant language doesn't arise in the same way. But it does arise!

And it does so in small countries as well as large ones. To return to the case of Icelandic, spoken by fewer than 300,000 people, the elements of the problem seem simple. All the inhabitants of the island speak their own language among themselves, but when it comes to contacts with foreigners a good knowledge of English is desirable. Each language seems to have its own well-defined space. There is no external rivalry, since Icelandic has never been a language used in international communications, and no internal rivalry either, since no Icelandic mother would dream of talking to her son in English.

But things get more complicated when it comes to the vast area of access to knowledge. Iceland has to keep up a constant and costly effort to ensure that its young people go on reading in Icelandic, rather than in English, material first published in the rest of the world. If the government relaxed its vigilance and just let market forces and the power of numbers have it all their own way, the national language would soon be used for domestic purposes only. Its territory would shrink, and Icelandic would end up as a mere local dialect. If it is to remain a language in the full sense of the word, the best policy is not to embark upon a struggle, doomed in advance, against English, but rather to involve everyone in the task of, on the one hand, maintaining and developing the national language, and on the other, maintaining and strengthening relations with other languages.

If you try to tour Icelandic sites on the Internet — they must, incidentally, be the most numerous in the world in proportion to the size of the population — you notice three things. They are practically all in Icelandic; from most of them you can click on to a version in English; and several also offer a third language, often Danish or German. Personally I'd like to see them offer even more languages, chosen more systematically; but so far so good.

But while it is obvious that a good knowledge of English is necessary now for anyone wanting to communicate with the world as a whole, it is equally undeniable that English alone is not enough. Even if it fulfils completely some of our current needs, there are others that it does not satisfy. In particular, the need for identity.

For the Americans, the English and some others, the English language is of course the language of identity. But for the rest of mankind, that is to say more than nine-tenths of our contemporaries, it cannot fill that role, and it would be dangerous to try to make it do so unless we want to produce hordes of people who are unhinged and disoriented, with personalities that are unbalanced. No one should be forced to become a mental expatriate every time he opens a book, sits down in front of a screen, enters into a discussion, or thinks. People ought to be able to make their own modernity instead of always feeling they are borrowing it from others.

Moreover, and this in my view is the aspect of the matter that most needs to be stressed nowadays, even the language of identity plus the global language are no longer enough. Anyone with the means, the age and the abilities to do so ought to go further.

If a Frenchman and a Korean can speak, discuss things and do business together in English when they meet, that is no doubt an improvement on the past. But if a Frenchman and an Italian can talk to one another in English only, that is definitely a regression and an impoverishment of their relationship.

It's an excellent thing if many of the readers in a library in Madrid can enjoy Faulkner or Steinbeck in the original English. But it would be a matter for regret if a day came when nobody there could read the works of Flaubert, Musil, Pushkin or Strindberg alike in the languages in which they were written.

It seems to me that, contrary to what appearances may seem to suggest, we would be acting against the spirit of our age if we restricted ourselves to just the minimum number of languages regarded as absolutely necessary. Between the language of identity and the global language there stretches a vast space that we must learn how to bridge.

This time, to illustrate my argument, I shall choose a complex example, very fraught with consequences. The European Union is a group of countries, each of which has had a history and cultural influence of its own, and which have undertaken the task of making their futures converge. What will they be 50 years from now? A federation? A confederation? Irreversibly joined, or each going its own way? Will the Union expand towards Eastern Europe or the Mediterranean? How far will its limits stretch? Will it take in the Balkans? The countries of North Africa? Turkey? The Middle East? The Caucasus? On the answer to these questions depend many things in the world of tomorrow, in particular the relations between various civilisations and religions: Christianity, Islam and Judaism. But whatever the future of Europe, whatever form the Union adopts and whatever countries are included among its members, one question presents itself now and will still present itself to future generations: how are all the scores of human languages to be managed?

In other areas we do our best to unify, align and standardise, but in this connection we are very cautious. It may well be that tomorrow we shall have not only a common currency and unified legislation but also one army, one police and one government. But as soon as anyone attempts to whisk away the most Lilliputian of languages he unleashes the most passionate and unbridled reactions. So to avoid trouble we prefer to translate and translate ad infinitum, however much it costs.

But meanwhile a de facto unification is taking place. No one decided on it; many are annoyed by it; but everyday realities cannot be denied. Whenever an Italian, a German, a Swede and a Belgian have a drink together, whether they are students, journalists, businessmen, trade unionists or government officials, they are obliged to use a common language. If the European Union had been created 100 or even 50 years ago, that language would have been French. Today it is English.

Can we reconcile indefinitely these two imperatives: the desire to preserve every individual's special identity and the need for Europeans to be able to communicate with one another all the time and as freely as possible? We cannot leave it to time to solve the dilemma and prevent people from engaging, a few years hence, in bitter and fruitless linguistic conflicts. We know all too well what time will do.

The only possible answer is a voluntary policy aimed at strengthening linguistic diversity and based on a simple idea:

IN THE NAME OF IDENTITY

nowadays everybody obviously needs three languages. The first is his language of identity; the third is English. Between the two we have to promote a third language, freely chosen, which will often but not always be another European language. This will be for everyone the main foreign language taught at school, but it will also be much more than that — the language of the heart, the adopted language, the language you have married, the language you love.

Will future relations between Germany and France be in the hands of Anglophones from both countries, or of Frenchspeaking Germans and German-speaking Frenchmen? There ought to be no doubt about the answer. And the relations between Spain and Italy? And between all the members of the European Union? A little common sense, lucidity and willpower should be enough to ensure that commercial, cultural and other exchanges remain chiefly in the hands of those with a special interest in their opposite numbers; an interest they have demonstrated by a meaningful cultural investment, such as familiarising themselves with their interlocutors' language of identity. Only people like that can carry the relationship further.

This would mean that in the years to come we would have not only "general practitioners," knowing only their own language and English, but also "specialists," who, in addition to that basic equipment, would have their own special language for communication, freely chosen in accordance with their own affinities, and through which they would attain personal and professional fulfilment. It will always be a serious handicap not to know English, but it will also, more and more, be a serious handicap to know English only. And this will apply equally to those for whom English is the mother tongue.

To preserve the language of one's own identity, and never let it be so neglected that those who speak it have to turn elsewhere for access to what is offered them by the civilisation of today; to make the teaching of English as a third language a matter of course everywhere, and this without repining, but explaining to the younger generation that while it is necessary it is not sufficient; and at the same time to encourage linguistic diversity so that there are many people in every country familiar not only with Spanish, French, Portuguese, German but also with Arabic, Chinese, Japanese and a hundred other languages that are more rarely studied, and so even more valuable both to the individual student and to the community — such measures seem to me to constitute a wise policy for us to adopt if we want the fantastic current expansion in communications to bring us enrichment at all levels, rather than impoverishment, general mistrust and troubled minds.

I do not deny that my recommendations for preserving cultural diversity call for a certain amount of effort. But if we were to let ourselves off this task and just let things take their course; if the world civilisation taking shape before our eyes were to go on seeming essentially American, Anglophone or even occidental; then I think everybody would lose by it. The United States, because they would alienate a large part of the rest of the world, which already chafes at the present imbalance of power; the members of non-Western cultures, because they would gradually lose all that makes up their raison d'être and find themselves caught up in a rebellion doomed to failure; and, perhaps above all, Europe, which would lose on both counts, because while becoming the primary target of all who felt excluded, it would also be unable to maintain its own cultural and linguistic diversity.

4

I ALMOST GAVE THIS BOOK A SUBTITLE: How to tame the panther. Why "panther"? Because a panther kills if you persecute it and kills if you leave it alone, and the worst thing you can do is to leave it alone after you've wounded it. But also because a panther can be tamed.

This is more or less what I set out to say in this book on the subject of the desire for identity. It is not to be dealt with either by persecution or indulgence. It needs to be observed, studied calmly, understood, and then conquered and tamed if we don't want the world to become a jungle, or the future to resemble the worst images of the past, or our sons to have to look on as helplessly in 50 years' time as we do now at massacres, expulsions and other "cleansings" — to look on at them, and perhaps even to be their victims.

I have made it my business, every time I felt it was necessary, to say how the "panther" can be kept under control. Not that I'm authorised to do so by being privy to any special truths. It's just that it would not have been responsible, when considering this question, to set down nothing but hopes and exhortations. It was also incumbent upon me to point out paths that seem promising and distinguish them from those that appear to be dead ends.

But this book is not supposed to be a list of remedies. When you are dealing with such complex and varied facts you are unlikely to find a formula that fits every country regardless. I use the word "formula" advisedly. In Lebanon it is always cropping up in conversations about how power may be shared among the many different religious communities. Ever since I was a child I have heard the word repeated all around me, in English, in French, and above all in the Arabic, *sigha,* an expression suggesting some kind of complicated work in silver or gold.

I could spend a long time describing the peculiarities of the "Lebanese formula," but for the present purpose I shall dwell only on what is the least idiosyncratic, though it is also the most revealing, thing about it and the one most useful as an example. This feature is not the list of Lebanon's 20 or so communities — still known as "confessions" — with their individual histories, their age-old fears, their bloody quarrels and amazing reconciliations. It is simply the fundamental idea of ensuring a stable equilibrium through a meticulous system of quotas.

When the inhabitants of a country all feel they belong to different communities — religious, linguistic, ethnic, racial, tribal or whatever — how can this state of affairs be "managed"? Should all the different allegiances be taken into account? If so, to what extent? Or should they be ignored, treated as if they were invisible?

There is a wide range of possible answers to this question. The one arrived at by the founders of modern Lebanon is certainly extreme. Its formal recognition of the many communities is worthy of respect, but the way it puts this recognition into practice is excessive. It could have set an example, but it has become a warning rather than a model. This is largely because of the complexities of Middle Eastern reality, but partly too because of the deficiencies of the formula itself, with its inflexibility, pitfalls and inconsistencies.

But for all that the experiment as a whole is not to be disparaged. I have said it was worthy of respect because it is laudable to have made a place for every community instead of giving all the power to just one of them and condemning the rest to submit or disappear. It is laudable to have worked out a system of subtle checks and balances that has allowed liberties to develop and the arts to flourish in a region where most other countries have a single religion, a single ideology, a single party or a single language, and where those who don't have the good fortune to be born on the right side of the communal barrier have no alternative but submission, exile or death. For all these reasons I still say, and shall go on saying, that despite its failures the Lebanese experiment is in my opinion more honourable than other experiments in the Middle East and elsewhere which have not, or not yet, produced a civil war but which have built their relative stability on repression, oppression, surreptitious "cleansing" and de facto discrimination.

So, though based on a worthy idea, the Lebanese formula went astray in its application: a deviation that might be called exemplary in the sense that it demonstrates the limits of the quota system and of all attempts at unity through community.

The main concern of those who thought up the Lebanese formula was to avoid elections in which a Christian and a Muslim candidate might come face to face and be automatically backed up by their respective communities, each supporting its own "son." The solution adopted was to divide up the various available posts in advance, so that instead of the confrontation occurring between two different communities it took place between candidates belonging to the same community. In theory, a neat and sensible idea. But when it came to be applied at all levels of government, from the presidency of the republic to the parliament and the civil service, what actually happened was that every important post became the "property" of one particular community!

When I was young I often fulminated against the absurdity of a system which, instead of choosing the more competent of two candidates for a job, appointed the one whose community had a "right" to it. Even now, when the occasion arises, I react in the same way. The only difference is that when I was 19 I would have been ready to replace the system by anything, whereas at 49 I'd still like to change it but not to put just any old thing in its place.

When I say that, I'm thinking of other places besides Lebanon. If the system there has turned out to have some perverse effects, that is not to say we should draw conclusions that are more perverse still — such, for example, as to think that societies made up of several different communities "are not made for democracy," and that only governments using strong-arm tactics can make them live in peace.

One even hears some democrats saying that sort of thing, claiming to be "realistic" despite the disavowals adduced by events of recent years. If democracy cannot always manage to solve "ethnic" problems, that doesn't mean dictatorship has done any better. Was the one-party Yugoslav regime any more successful at keeping domestic peace than the multiparty system in Lebanon? Marshal Tito might 30 years ago have seemed a lesser evil because the outer world didn't see different ethnic groups killing one another anymore. But now we realise that none of the fundamental problems was solved. Far from it.

What has recently happened in most countries belonging to the former communist world is so vivid in our minds that there is no need to describe it at length. But perhaps it is worth stressing that governments which suppress democracy in fact reinforce traditional allegiances. When a society is riddled with suspicion, the last solidarities to survive are the most visceral ones: when all political, trade union and academic freedoms have been shackled, religious assemblies become the only places where people can gather together, talk and feel united in the face of adversity. Many people have entered the Soviet universe as "proletarians" and left it more "religious" and "nationalist" than ever. With the passage of time, so-called "secular" dictatorships emerge as nurseries of religious fanaticism. Secularism without democracy is a disaster for democracy and secularism alike.

But there is no need to press the point further. For anyone who aspires to a world of liberty and justice, dictatorship cannot be an acceptable solution: there is no point in going into its obvious inability to solve problems related to religious and ethnic affiliation or to identity. It is only in the context of democracy that the question of choice arises.

But that doesn't get us very far. Just saying the word "democracy" isn't enough to create peaceful coexistence. There are democracies and democracies, and the excesses committed by some of them are no less lethal than those perpetrated by dictatorships. There are two courses that seem to me to hold special dangers, not only for cultural diversity but also for the basic principles of democracy itself. One is of course the quota system carried to ridiculous extremes; the other is its opposite: a system that respects only the law of numbers, without any safeguards.

Lebanon is clearly a particularly revealing example of the first option, though it isn't the only one. There power is divided up among the different communities — temporarily, we are told — in the hope of lessening tensions and of gradually getting everyone to feel they belong to a "national community." But the system by its very nature produces a quite different result: as soon as it comes to the cutting of the "cake," each community tends to feel that it is getting too small a slice and is the victim of flagrant injustice. And some politicians exploit this resentment and make it a main plank in their propaganda.

Little by little the leaders who refrain from sensationalism find themselves marginalised. Then, instead of lessening, the sense of belonging to different "tribes" grows stronger, while the sense of belonging to the national community weakens until it disappears, or almost. Always amid bitterness; sometimes in a bloodbath. If you are in Europe, you get Belgium; if you are in the Middle East, you get Lebanon.

I am oversimplifying a little, but in the matter of "ethnic" problems this is the scenario you head for as soon as community allegiances are allowed to turn into substitutes for individual identity instead of being incorporated into a single wider, redefined national identity.

The recognition of linguistic, religious, regional and other special allegiances within the national collectivity can often alleviate tensions and improve relations among the various groups of citizens. But it is a delicate process, not to be embarked on lightly, for all too easily something can make it produce the opposite of the desired effect. In one instance the authorities took steps to encourage the integration of a minority community, only to discover, 20 years later, that its members had merely been inescapably confined in a ghetto. Instead of lightening the atmosphere among the different groups of citizens, the government had created a system of fierce rivalries, recriminations and demands which could not be stemmed and which politicians had made their raison d'être and stock-in-trade.

Any kind of discrimination is dangerous, even if it is meant to help a community that has suffered. This is not only because it replaces one injustice by another, thus increasing hatred and suspicion, but also because of a principle that I consider even more serious. As long as an individual's place in society goes on depending on his belonging to some community or another we are perpetuating a perverse state of affairs that can only deepen divisions. If we want to reduce inequalities and injustices and racial, ethnic, religious and other tensions, the only reasonable and decent policy is to work to ensure that every citizen is treated as a fully-fledged member of society, whatever his affiliations. Of course, such a destination cannot be reached from one day to the next, but that is no reason for driving in the opposite direction.

5

THE DEFECTS OF THE QUOTA and the "unity through community" systems have resulted in so many tragedies all over the world that they seem to justify the opposite attitude, which prefers to ignore differences and rely in every case on the supposedly infallible judgement of the majority.

At first sight such a position seems to reflect pure democratic good sense: we don't need to know that the citizens of a society include Muslims, Jews, Christians, Blacks, Asians, Hispanics, Walloons and Flemings — each of them has a vote, and there is no better law than that establishing universal suffrage! The only trouble with this venerable "law" is that as soon as there are clouds in the sky it doesn't work anymore. In Germany, in the early 1920s, universal suffrage served to create government coalitions that reflected public opinion. But in the early 1930s that same universal suffrage, exercised in an atmosphere coloured by acute social crisis and racist propaganda, led to the abolition of democracy. By the time the German people could again express themselves freely, millions of people had died. The law of the majority is not always synonymous with democracy, liberty and equality. Sometimes it is synonymous with tyranny, slavery and discrimination.

Where there is an oppressed minority a free vote doesn't necessarily set it free. It may even make the oppression worse. You would need to be very naive — or very cynical — to maintain that by giving power to a majority faction you decrease the sufferings of minorities. In Rwanda it is estimated that the Hutus represent about nine-tenths of the population, and the Tutsis one tenth. A "free" vote now would be no more than an ethnic census, and if the authorities tried to apply majority law there without any safeguards, the result would inevitably be a massacre or a dictatorship.

I haven't quoted this example by chance. If you examine closely the political debate that accompanied the 1994 massacres, you see that the fanatics always claimed to act in the name of democracy. They even went so far as to compare their rebellion to the French Revolution of 1789, and the extermination of the Tutsis to the elimination by Robespierre and his friends of a privileged caste. Some Catholic priests were even persuaded that they should range themselves "on the side of the poor" and so far "understand the anger of the poor" as to act as accomplices in genocide.

Such arguments make me uneasy, not only because they try to glorify the contemptible actions of cutthroats, but also because they show how the most noble of principles may be hijacked. Ethnic massacres are always backed up by fine excuses — justice, equality, independence, the rights of the people, democracy, the fight against privilege and so on.

Events in various countries over the past few years should teach us to be wary whenever an allegedly universal idea is pressed into service in a conflict over identity.

Some of the human communities who suffer discrimination are in the majority in their countries, as was the case in South Africa until apartheid was abolished. But usually it is minorities who suffer, who are deprived of their most elementary rights and who live in constant terror and humiliation. If you live in a country where you are afraid to admit that your name is Pierre, or Mahmoud, or Baruch, and where that state of affairs has lasted for four or perhaps for 40 generations; if you live in a country where you don't even need to make such an "admission" because your allegiance is to be seen in the colour of your face, because you are a member of what in some places is called the "visible minorities" — if you live under any of these conditions, you don't need long explanations to convince you that the words "majority" and "minority" don't always belong to the vocabulary of democracy.

Before one can speak of democracy, public debate must be able to take place in an atmosphere of relative calm. For an election to be meaningful, a vote that has people's own opinions behind it — the only kind of vote that is free — must have replaced the automatic vote, the ethnic vote, the fanatical vote, and the vote dictated by identity. Whenever the political climate becomes racist, totalitarian or based on the notion of unity through community, the role of democrats everywhere is no longer to support the preferences of the majority but to see that the rights of the oppressed are respected, if necessary in the face of numerical superiority.

What is sacred in democracy is not mechanisms but values. What must be respected, absolutely and without concession, is the dignity of human beings — all human beings, men, women and children, whatever their beliefs or their colour, and whether they are many or few. The voting system must take all these requirements into account.

If universal suffrage can be adopted without involving too much injustice, so much the better. Otherwise, safeguards need to be put in place. The main democracies all have recourse to such precautions at one time or another. In the United Kingdom, majority voting reigns supreme, but faced with the problem of the Catholic minority in Northern Ireland, the UK has devised other electoral systems that do not depend entirely on strict majority rule. France, in order to deal with the particular problem of Corsica, has recently introduced a regional vote different from that in the rest of the country. In the United States, Rhode Island, a state with a million inhabitants, has two senators, the same number as California, which has 30 million inhabitants: an infringement of the principle of majority rule, introduced by the founding fathers to stop the larger states from crushing the weaker ones.

But I'd like to return briefly to South Africa, where the use of the slogan "majority rule" might lead to confusion. In the context of apartheid the phrase was a comprehensible abbreviation so long as those who used it made it clear — as did men like Nelson Mandela — that the object was not to replace a white government by a black one, nor to substitute one state of discrimination for another, but to give all citizens, whatever their origins, the same political rights, after which it would be up to them to elect the leaders of their choice, whether those leaders themselves were of African, European, Asian or mixed descent.

There is nothing to stop us supposing that one day a black person might be elected president of the United States and a white person president of the "new" South Africa. But neither eventuality is likely until an effective process exists, aimed at promoting domestic harmonisation, integration and maturity, by which time each candidate can at last be judged by his fellow-citizens on the basis of his human qualities and his opinions and not of his inherited allegiances. It goes without saying that we have not reached that point yet. No one has, anywhere, to tell the truth. Not the United States, not South Africa, nor any other country. Things are better in some places than in others, but nowhere on the whole map of the world can I find a single country where the religious and ethnic affiliations of all the candidates is regarded by the voters as irrelevant.

Even in the oldest democracies there are still inconsistencies. I think it would still be difficult for a professed Roman Catholic to be prime minister in London. In France there is no longer any prejudice against the Protestant minority: all its members, whether believers or not, can offer themselves as candidates for the highest posts in the state, and the voters will take into account only their personal merits and political opinions. On the other hand, none of the 600 or so mainland constituencies has yet elected a Muslim to the Assemblée Nationale. Elections do no more than reflect the image a society has of itself and of its component parts. They may help it arrive at a diagnosis, but they alone can never produce a cure.

Perhaps I should not have dwelt so long in the last few pages on Lebanon, Rwanda, South Africa and the former Yugoslavia. The dramas that have steeped those countries in blood in recent decades have been so much in the news that all other tensions might seem mild in comparison, and even negligible. But there isn't a country in the world today that doesn't need to ponder on how to get different populations, local or immigrant, to live together. Everywhere there are tensions more or less skilfully contained; usually they show signs of getting worse. And the problem often presents itself simultaneously on many different levels. In Europe, for example, most states have to confront some regional and linguistic problems, as well as others linked to the presence of immigrant communities, and also "continental" problems which may not be very acute now but which will become increasingly evident as more and more countries are brought into the Union. For then it will be necessary to organise a "life in common" for some 20 or 30 nations, each with its own history, language and susceptibilities.

Of course we must keep a sense of proportion. Not all fevers are symptoms of the plague. But neither should any of them be dismissed with a shrug of the shoulders. Don't we worry about a flu epidemic and keep a close watch on the evolution of the virus concerned?

Needless to say, different patients require different treatment. In some cases institutional safeguards need to be introduced, and sometimes, in countries with a "bad previous history," the international community needs to supply some active supervision to prevent discrimination and slaughter and preserve cultural diversity. Most other countries will require no more than subtle correctives, aimed chiefly at improving the social and intellectual atmosphere. But everywhere there is a need for calm and thorough reflection on the best way to tame the wild beast of identity.

Epilogue

*T*HOSE READERS WHO HAVE STAYED WITH ME SO FAR won't be surprised to find me expressing the opinion that the argument with which we have been concerned needs to start out from one central idea: that every individual should be able to identify, at least to some degree, both with the country he lives in and with our present-day world. This involves the adoption of certain habits and types of behaviour, not only by the individual himself, but also by the people around him, whether groups or other individuals.

Each of us should be encouraged to accept his own diversity, to see his identity as the sum of all his various affiliations, instead of as only one of them raised to the status of the most important, made into an instrument of exclusion and sometimes into a weapon of war. Especially in the case of those whose culture of origin is not that of the society they live in, people must be able to accept a dual affiliation without too much anguish; which means remaining loyal to their culture of origin and not feeling obliged to conceal it like some shameful disease, and at the same time being receptive to the culture of their adoptive country.

Formulated like this, the precept seems to apply mainly to migrants, but in fact it also concerns those who have always lived in a society other than that of their ancestors but who are still emotionally linked to their culture of origin. I am thinking, for example, of black people in the United States. The phrase currently applied to them — African Americans — reflects their dual allegiance. But my precept is equally relevant to all those who for religious, ethnic, social or other reasons, feel "minoritised" and set apart in the only mother country they have ever known. For all of them, the ability to live easily with their various allegiances is essential not only for their own fulfilment, but also for the peace of the society of which they are part.

In the same way, societies themselves need to accept the many affiliations that have forged each of their collective identities in the course of history, and that are shaping them still. They ought to make the necessary effort to demonstrate by means of visible symbols that they accept their own identities, so that every individual may identify with what he sees around him, may recognise himself in the image of the country in which he lives, and may feel encouraged to involve himself in it rather than, as is too often the case, remaining an uneasy and sometimes hostile spectator.

Naturally, not all a country's affiliations are of equal importance. I am not preaching a meaningless sham equality, but rather the acceptance of a multiplicity of allegiances as all equally legitimate. For example, France's main religious tradition is obviously Catholic, but this should not prevent the

country from acknowledging that it also has a Protestant, a
Jewish and a Muslim dimension, not to mention a Voltairean
one that is profoundly suspicious of all religions. Each of
these dimensions — and the list is not exhaustive — has
played and still does play a significant part in the life of the
country and in its fundamental perception of its own identity.

Moreover, there can be no doubt that the French language, too, has an identity derived from many different affiliations. Latin first and foremost, but German also, and Celtic,
together with African, West Indian, Arabic, Slav and other
more recent contributions which enrich it without necessarily adulterating it.

I have quoted only the case of France, a subject upon
which I could of course have spoken at greater length. But
every society has its own special vision of itself and of its own
identity. The countries of the New World, and in particular
the United States, have no difficulty in admitting that their
identity is made up of many different affiliations, since they
were created out of the contributions of immigrants from
all over the world. But these migrants did not all arrive in the
same circumstances. Some came in search of a better life;
others had been abducted and brought there against their will.
Only after a long, a very long and difficult process, not yet
complete, will these sons of immigrants, together with the
descendants of those already living there in the pre-Columbian
period, all be able to identify fully with the society they live in.
But here the problem consists not so much in the principle of
diversity itself as in how to put it into practice.

Elsewhere, the question of identity presents itself differently. In Western Europe, which has in fact become a receiver

of immigrants although it did not see itself in that role, some peoples still find it difficult to apprehend their identity in terms of any other culture but their own. This is true above all of peoples who have long been divided or deprived of independence. Their historical continuity is not based on a national territory and a state of their own, but on cultural and ethnic bonds. That said, Europe too, taken as a whole and insofar as it tends towards unity, certainly ought to see its own identity as the sum of all its linguistic, religious and other affiliations. If it does not accept every element in its history, if it fails to impress on its future citizens that they must learn to feel fully European without ceasing to be German or French or Italian or Greek, it will simply not be able to exist.

Creating a new Europe means creating a new concept of identity, for Europe itself, for all the countries in it, and to a certain extent for the rest of the world too.

Much could be said of this example, as of that of America and many others. But I shall resist the temptation to go into detail and just deal with a single aspect — in my view an important one — of the "functioning" of identity: the way it works. As soon as someone decides to belong to a country or group of countries such as a united Europe, he can't help feeling a certain kinship with all its component parts. Of course, he still has a very special relationship with his own culture and feels a certain responsibility towards it, but at the same time he builds up relations with the other components of the adopted country or group of countries. As soon as a Piedmontese feels Italian, he is bound to take an interest in the history of Venice or Naples, even if he still has a special affection for Turin and its past. Similarly, the more this same

Italian feels European, the more he will be interested in the histories of Amsterdam and Lübeck, and they will seem less and less alien to him. All this may take two or three generations, a bit longer in some cases. But I know some young Europeans who already behave as if the whole continent were their homeland and all its inhabitants their compatriots.

As someone who proclaims every one of his allegiances from the rooftops, I can't help dreaming of the day when the region where I was born will follow the path I have described, leaving behind the era of tribes, of holy wars and of identities that kill, in order to build something in common. I dream of the day when I can call all the Middle East my homeland, as I now do Lebanon and France and Europe; the day when I can call all its sons, Muslim, Jewish and Christian, of all denominations and all origins, my compatriots. In my own mind, which is always speculating and trying to anticipate the future, it has already come to pass. But I want it to happen one day on the solid ground of reality, and for everyone.

Reluctantly, I end this digression, to return to my original theme and to apply what I have already said about individual countries to the world as a whole. We must act in such a way as to bring about a situation in which no one feels excluded from the common civilisation that is coming into existence; in which everyone may be able to find the language of his own identity and some symbols of his own culture; and in which everyone can identify to some degree with what he sees emerging in the world about him, instead of seeking refuge in an idealised past.

In parallel to this, everyone should be able to include in what he regards as his own identity a new ingredient, one that will assume more and more importance in the course of the new century and the new millennium: the sense of belonging to the human adventure as well as his own.

That is more or less what I wanted to say about the wish for identity and about its lethal potentialities. I should have liked to deal exhaustively with the subject, but I have really only begun to scratch the surface. To each paragraph I have written I could have added 20 others. Rereading the book, I'm not sure I have managed to find the right tone (not too cool and not too passionate), the most convincing arguments, the best possible words. Never mind. All I wanted to do was throw out a few ideas, bear witness, and make others think about things that have always preoccupied me, and the more so the longer I have observed the fascinating and disconcerting world into which I was lucky enough to be born.

When an author reaches the last page of a book his fondest wish is usually that his work should still be read 100 or 200 years hence. You never can tell. Some books intended to be immortal expire immediately, while another, regarded as a schoolboy diversion, survives. But hope springs eternal.

For this book, neither a literary work nor a diversion, I make a different wish. May my grandson, growing up and finding it one day by chance on the family bookshelves, look through the pages, read a passage or two, then put it back in the dusty corner where he found it, shrugging his shoulders and marvelling that in his grandfather's day such things still needed to be said.